# CHILDREN, FEELINGS AND DIVORCE

# CHILDREN, FEELINGS AND DIVORCE

*Finding the Best Outcome*

HEATHER SMITH

FREE ASSOCIATION BOOKS / LONDON / NEW YORK

First published in Great Britain in 1999 by
FREE ASSOCIATION BOOKS
57 Warren Street, London W1P 5PA

A CIP catalogue record for this book is available
from the British Library

ISBN 1 85343 434 5 pbk

Designed, typeset and produced for the publisher by
Chase Production Services, Chadlington, OX7 5QR
Printed in the EC by J.W. Arrowsmith, Bristol

# Contents

# Acknowledgements

As this is a book which owes its existence to children it is them I have to thank first. Included are the many children who have shared their thoughts and feelings with me over many years and, more recently, those who I have seen on their own and in groups. I am especially grateful to the young people who had experienced a 'good divorce' and who were willing to talk to me. They, though small in number, made the whole project worthwhile.

I shall never cease to be grateful to Elizabeth James for her wisdom and encouragement over a number of years. The comments Tim Smith made about the chapters he read were also much appreciated and, in addition, I would like to thank Maria Kraithman for her support, as well as the Hertfordshire Family Mediation Service for enabling the groups for children to take place.

To Branwen Lucas I am greatly indebted on a number of counts: first, for reading some of the chapters and making some pertinent comments; second, because she was the original instigator of the groups and, as joint group leader, brought warmth, an intuitive understanding of children and an inventive mind to every group we have run together. Her kindness in sharing her expertise in several areas covered by this book was boundless and her interest and help during its inception invaluable.

Finally I have to give my heartfelt thanks to my husband, John, for his patience and help in countless ways over the last ten months, and for helping me through the times when I despaired.

# Preface

'... the unspoken but deeply felt and often neglected pain of children ... the simple heroism of children and their touching efforts at concealment, as though to shield grown ups from too much pain.' *Maurice Sendak*

## The Focus and Aims of this Book

Children quite naturally want their parents to live together happily and to be a 'normal' family approximating to the mum and dad plus children of so many stories. This book is about children for whom this is not a reality, for the many for whom the family provides a very different experience from the stereotype of happy families in which the child is untroubled by adult concerns. Their experiences at the time of divorce and readjustment to the changes in their life form the focus of this book.

What is it like for children? What might help them to recover well? My thinking about these matters has led to what is the core of this book: that divorce, or the separation of parents, although usually a painful experience for a child, does not have to be followed by disastrous consequences for the rest of a child's life; there is much that can be done to avoid long-term harm.

Although divorce is often blamed for whatever is troubling a child this can be a false conclusion; there is the time before and a time after the separation. The separation might be the catalyst which has caused the distress of the child prior to the event; alternatively, mishandling after the separation may be the direct cause. However, in the last twenty years it has become a major event in so many children's lives that it is important to try to understand the feelings and behaviour of the children involved.

The book is a personal statement. It is one person's view of a complex matter, a look at those parts of the divorce process and its outcomes which are difficult to evaluate or to ascertain by statistics. It is concerned with the intangible feelings aroused by a situation none of the participants foresaw or desired when they first married or lived together. As a result children are confused by a fusion of sadness and disappointment, love and loyalty, anxiety and anger, as well as those feelings which are a reaction to experiences and to relationships which have developed since babyhood. It is not only about what has been called 'giving sorrow words' but discusses many of the other stresses which lone parents, as well as children, might face. The words of many different children are referred to and quoted but in order to preserve confidentiality, all names have been changed and family circumstances disguised.

There is very little reference to the feelings of children who live with their fathers. I am aware that this is a serious omission; the reason for it is quite simply my lack of experience of talking to children in this situation. It is certainly an area which needs exploring. Another gap is any reference, for the same reason, to children from ethnic minorities and step-families are mentioned briefly (Gorill Barnes 1998).

## Readership

It is hoped that the book will be of value to parents and to practitioners of every kind concerned with children, whether in education, social work, medicine, the legal profession or therapy. Most of it should be of interest to both groups, although some parts are addressed more specifically to one than to the other. The majority of chapters focus on children, but some are primarily concerned with parents and their feelings. A chapter directly addressed to children is included in the hope that children involved with their parents' separation may read it.

## Themes and Concepts

A number of themes derived from working with children in many different settings, as well as from the work of other writers, underlie this book. Over a long period it is difficult to distinguish what has been learnt by experience and what has been absorbed from others; it may be that some sources have long been forgotten, and if they are not acknowledged it is unintentional. Although books and articles have been used, no systematic search of the literature was undertaken. Sometimes conclusions arrived at independently have subsequently been found in other people's work, usually academics with a strongly theoretical background and engaged in a research project. Convergence of this kind, starting from quite different bases of experience, has been allowed to stand without comment, as being instructive (Smart and Neale 1998).

Central to the whole text is the belief that children's feelings are important and need to be considered far more than is generally the case; and that their opinions should be listened to and valued, especially when their parents separate. This is not a plea for them to be allowed to make decisions, only that they should contribute actively in reaching conclusions over matters that concern them. It is a comparatively new idea that they even have an opinion – grown-ups know best. 'They didn't ask what I thought', and, 'Nobody told me what was happening', are all too familiar phrases to those who work with children with separated parents.

Children feel emotional pain, especially where the most important people in their lives, their parents, are concerned. It can often be difficult for adults to understand the strength of their feelings because, first, they are demonstrated in a different way from their own and, second, many children are reluctant to express them. Why this should be will be discussed at some length. The film by James and Joyce Robinson, *A Two-year-old Goes to Hospital*, made about forty years ago, was something of a watershed in the way it demonstrated dramatically to those working with children the phases of distress that hospitalization caused a small child. Around that time too a French film, *Les jeux interdits* (Forbidden Games), demonstrated with great sensitivity children's attempts to come to terms with death. The belief that children's suffering is little more than transitory has been firmly held, one that does not clash with the conventional point of view so often expressed after separation. 'He's only a child, he'll soon get over it. They don't understand.' These words are used by some adults to protect themselves from having to deal with a bereft child.

These two themes, that children have opinions which are important to hear and that their unhappiness is not always appreciated, have several strands running through them. One is the assumption that every child has a number of basic needs. Briefly, these needs include:

unconditional love expressed in an age-appropriate way;

respect for the child's personality as well as what he does – in other words, for him to be valued and enjoyed;

adult time for shared activities, play and stimulus;

the stability necessary for the child to be able to predict events and the likely consequences of his actions;

that parents be in charge and provide benign limits within a framework of freedom;

and encouragement and help in maturing.

For children of divorce, one or two of these needs take a particular form arising from their situation. For them, respect means that they must be treated fairly and on an equal footing with the other children in the family, whether their own brothers and sisters or new children who join them. Stability acquires a special importance that can easily be endangered by fluid adult relationships endangering their wish for a caring family, and to be safe. These needs are not met if a child is harmed by any abuse, whether emotional, physical or sexual, or by neglect.

'Emotional abuse', a phrase used throughout the book, needs to be defined. It does not refer to a single specific incident but to a sustained belittling of a child's personality, ability or achievements, whether thoughtless or deliberate. Because there are no signs which make the abuse obvious it is often difficult to assess and therefore largely denied by those responsible. It takes place when parents' management of their child is unkind and damaging in a way which can be incomprehensible. When a child is brought up in this way her self-esteem is seriously undermined.

Children suffer emotional abuse from parents in many different ways. They may be ignored or ostracized, or have to listen to constant teasing or harmful criticism. Other abuse which betrays itself by few signs, except an unnatural wariness which leaves no marks, is experienced when children are disciplined by threats, fear or harsh punishments and by those who are given unsuitable responsibilities (Smith 1995, Ch. 5). Emotional abuse related to divorce can take many forms including a child repeatedly hearing one parent making threats or detrimental remarks about the other or threatening harm to the child or other parent. Its recurrence forms a second strand and is accompanied by an important plea; that emotional abuse should be given far more prominence when decisions regarding children are being considered. At present the plight of a great number of unhappy children is ignored.

A third strand is the belief, too often ignored in research in this subject, that good experiences contribute to reducing the negative effects of stressful events, which carries the hopeful message that for children whose parents separate, it is never too late to make changes for the good. If this is accepted, what follows is that the experience of divorce for children does not have to be 'a life sentence' as many parents fear and as all too often happens; in fact much harm that is being done is avoidable. If this book makes even a small contribution to increasing the awareness of the pain of children and helps to add to the number who can say that, for them, it was a 'good divorce', it will have achieved its purpose.

## A Brief Outline

Before discussing children's feelings about the separation it is appropriate briefly to consider marriage and the reasons for marital breakdown; this is the subject of Chapter 1. Chapter 2 discusses some of the issues at the time of separation and is followed by two chapters on how children react and what they might feel about the event. Chapters 5 and 6 are concerned with domestic violence and are followed by two chapters on methods of helping children in this situation, including children's groups. Chapters 10 to 12 relate more to parents and discuss living apart, the difficulties of contact, and mediation. Chapter 13 deals with children and mediation; Chapter 14 is addressed directly to children; and the whole is rounded off with a conclusion.

## Vocabulary

Three points need to be made about the vocabulary used. First, *separation*, used here generally in preference to divorce, refers to the increasing number of parents who separate after an initial shared relationship: some are married and divorced; others not; but in all cases children are involved. Exactly how many children are affected is not known because unmarried parents who live together, however long their relationship may have lasted, are not included in the statistics. However, it is known that in recent years there has been a ten-fold increase in cohabitation; that one in three children today are born outside marriage; and that a considerable number of children have experienced multiple changes in the constitution of their family.

The second point relates to the *gender of the resident parent*; readers here might be led to think that, following separation, children live only with their mother. In fact, nearly one in five of all children live with one parent (1996 figures) and, with the exception of about 14 per cent who live with their father, the mother is the resident parent. Although many of the comments refer to either parent, with the exception of what is written about lone fathers in Chapter 10 the word *mother* is generally used when referring to the resident parent for the sake of avoiding clumsiness in style.

The third point relates to gender-specific pronouns when referring to 'the child'. Masculine and feminine pronouns are used more or less indiscriminately throughout the book to avoid the awkwardness of 'he/she', 'his/her', and so on.

A final comment. Although professional people unquestionably know a great deal about children overall and are keenly aware of the diversity of reactions to parental separation, nevertheless it is the parents who know their own child best. They are likely to have some understanding of the multiple factors that went to produce his unique situation as well as the events which have shaped the child's life from the beginning. The child's personality and his tremendous drive towards growth and health as well as his survival strategies could also be appreciated by them. It is relationships in the family, including the extended family, and the degree of care and closeness between individual members that can play a crucial part in arriving at a good outcome. There is a lot for parents – and others – to understand.

## The Author

Most of my career has been spent working with children in different settings including comparatively brief spells in youth clubs and at a residential children's home; this was followed by a longer period as a school teacher. The really formative period of my career was my work in Child and Family Clinics, in one of which I was a senior clinic social worker, and it was there, while working with a child psychiatrist who had a profound understanding of children, that my views began to take shape. For the last eight years I have been a voluntary mediator but latterly have spent more time, with another group leader, in running groups for children who come not because they have an emotional problem but because their parents have separated. My first book, largely based on my clinical experience, was called *Unhappy Children: Reasons and Remedies*, and it was published by Free Association Books in 1995.

# 1 Introduction: Marriages Which End in Separation

## A Difficult Decision

Marriage in itself is not the subject of this book, but some consideration of it is inseparable from the problems it produces for children
involved in its break-up. What follows is an outline of some of the
reasons likely to underlie marital difficulties encountered by counsellors and which form the background to many of the divorces involving
children. It is based on personal experience and is neither a systematic
survey nor is it concerned to provide solutions; it merely provides a
backdrop to the problems which culminate in separation and often
continue after it, problems which children are generally aware of, even
though they may not always perceive their causes.

All separated parents wanted and expected to have a happy
marriage and many have reluctantly had to give up hope that the
breakdown is not permanent. Despite the magnitude of the problems
which almost inevitably occur as a consequence of separation,
including the lack of money and the stress of having the main
responsibility for the children's upbringing and welfare, seven out of
ten divorces are initiated by women. We might wonder why so many
find their marriages intolerable and embark on a course which can
increase their difficulties, at least in the short term. Many do so only
after repeated attempts at reconciliation.

The average duration of a marriage is rather less than ten years and
for those in a non-marital relationship the duration is even less; as a
result the proportion of young children who experience the separation
of their parents is high. A fairly general pattern is for one partner to
leave and return, perhaps a number of times, before the final break and
often after counselling or contacting Relate (the marriage guidance
service), and from this it is clear that the decision to separate is usually
not made lightly, especially if there are children to consider. We can
assume that there are very powerful considerations to weigh up before
arriving at so painful a decision – one which is unlikely to be affected
by making divorce a longer process and more difficult to obtain. The
emotional energy which formed a large part of a person's self and

identity is likely to have been invested in the marriage, making it hard to surrender and start what can seem like a new life.


## Influences of Society

A change in the status of women, an increasing desire for emotional satisfaction, social pressures related to the transitory nature of much of our culture, and, perhaps the most important, the instability of the labour market – these are influences which have contributed to a revolutionary change in the institution of marriage over the last fifty years. Wives now are no longer seen, as they were in the past, to be subservient to their husbands, or even in charge of their own separate domain – the house and the children – while their husbands provide the families' links with the wider world. In many marriages and relationships the expectation is of more equal status with both partners working and both involved in childcare, though not often on an equal basis. Preserving the stability of the relationship is no longer the prime consideration; instead, emotional satisfaction is considered more important, especially the sexual relationship. Nothing is expected to last long, neither jobs nor possessions, and often, sadly for the children involved, not marriage.

Today marriages and partnerships are entered into in the belief that they can be ended easily. Certainly there is far less of the social stigma which was formerly attached to separation; cohabitation is socially acceptable, even fashionable. However, with the growing awareness that children are affected by the break-up, the emotional stress is generally greater because of concern about the children's feelings. The change is made harder for all concerned by the fact that the extended family is less likely to be available than previously.


## Patterns in Relationships

Despite growing acceptance of the idea that children can be affected by the separation of their parents, there is as yet not much understanding by the general public of the myriad reasons for the failure of marriages. Two of the many patterns of marriage break-up are related to the unequal distribution of power in the relationship. One pattern is parental in character; that is, one spouse behaves like a parent of a naughty child (Clulow and Vincent 1987). In this situation both spouses may have been happy with their respective roles until the arrival of children, at which time the risk of difficulties arose unless they were able to make suitable changes that were equally acceptable to both of them. The second marital pattern is one which is potentially more dangerous, both emotionally and physically, for children; it is where power is unequal and one partner is afraid of the other, a situation discussed in Chapter 5.

The expectations of married couples have also changed. In the past marriage gave a woman a higher status than that of her single sisters, leading, inevitably for most, to motherhood. For a man it was also a rite of passage; he had ended his apprenticeship and now had to accept the responsibilities of being the head of his own household. The sexual relationship was obviously important, but was not necessarily the primary consideration. In contrast, today it is this aspect which is probably the start of the process and the current wish for sharing and companionship is not given a great deal of consideration – it is certainly not seen as something which might prove difficult in the future.

## Influences from Childhood

Understanding the reasons why marriages fail involves having some grasp of the emotional problems left over from childhood, because they continue to have a powerful influence on how people behave towards each other, especially in close relationships. All couples bring something of their childhood experiences into the new relationship, whether it is by repeating patterns, attempting not to repeat them, or trying to meet needs which were not satisfactorily dealt with when they were children.

Although an increase in teenage pregnancies is cause for concern, early marriages – which, despite popular belief, do not always end in disaster – can nevertheless be a more obvious way than most of attempting to solve problems stemming from childhood. A common instance is one in which a very strong need exists for a loving relationship, causing one of the couple to see the partner in the way that fulfils this need, not as he or she is in reality. These couples embark on marriage and parenthood without really knowing each other and have unrealistic expectations of the relationship.

A woman brought up in fear of her father may over-react with apprehension when her partner shouts; a man rejected by his mother as a child will be exceptionally sensitive to any comment which undermines his fragile confidence. Thus a crucial question for both partners is: 'What are the unresolved feelings from childhood which are affecting your attitude to your partner, or your response to what is happening or said?' This is a difficult matter which can involve looking at painful issues and some people may need the help of a counsellor in sorting them out, but to gain such understanding can lead to changes in relationships. It might involve acknowledging that both contributed to the difficulties, though rarely in equal portions.

## The Present: The Influence of Children

Although children are not the primary cause of marital disharmony, they can sometimes be a secondary one because of factors beyond their control. One such factor relates to a perceived imbalance between family members. A husband can be punitive to a child, not because he or she was naughty, but because he believed his wife was too lenient. Or a parent identifying with a child may be a cause. A wife sees one child, with whom she identifies strongly, as very special – an attachment that leads her to treat the child differently from the others in the family; to which the husband responds by treating another child as 'his'; or this is the third child and the father was the third child; this one was an ill baby who survived only because of the devotion of the mother and consequently is special to her; this one has red hair like the parent. The causes of identification can be deep-rooted but the reasons are usually not understood because the parents are so closely involved. Families like this are divided down the middle, a dichotomy which can lead to marital tensions. Divisions produced by these circumstances may cause children to show psychosomatic symptoms that provide further cause for misunderstanding. Of course, children are not simply victims of marital disharmony; they add their own contribution to the stresses in the family.

## Feelings Between Couples

Emotional taboos can be destructive to a relationship. Failure of a marriage can be founded on the fear that some feelings are too painful to be expressed openly, especially those relating to low self-esteem. These may stem from a lack of confidence in one's own worth or to a sense of failure in certain crucial areas of emotional life. Doubts of this kind may cause a spouse to fear that sharing them might have unwelcome consequences in the form of rejection or a reduction of his or her personal power to undermine the partner. For the latter, this creates an impenetrable barrier. In families like these it may be more acceptable to express anger than feelings of sadness or warmth;

though, for some, even anger cannot be expressed, and is demonstrated indirectly by silence and sulking. The children in the family may not understand exactly what the emotions are that they observe their parents unable to express, but they draw the conclusion that whatever they are, they cannot be displayed openly.

## The Distance Between Couples

Even where there is no absolute taboo on expressing emotions a mutual degree of closeness or distance is not found by everybody. A spouse who is unhappy in the relationship because the distance between the couple is too wide will soon begin to feel that the partner no longer cares, that nothing of importance is discussed and no activities are shared. Similarly, a failure to share affects the emotional satisfaction of the relationship and many spouses feel they are valued not for themselves but for what they do. Their role as bread-winner or housekeeper has become all-important.

For those in the opposite situation – finding the relationship too close, wanting the freedom to be independent and to engage in some individual activities – it is their partner's jealous feelings which are stifling; for them marriage is experienced as a trap. The delicate balance between separateness and closeness has been upset.

## Different Expectations

Marked differences in emotional maturity can lead to problems; one partner is concerned with the present, the other wants to plan ahead; one wants to settle down, perhaps to be like his or her parent, whereas the other is concerned to carry on enjoying life in the way the couple did before they were married; some are not ready to accept the long-term commitment of marriage, or are reluctant to make the compromises that are always necessary for a successful union. Different moral and religious beliefs and political convictions may not have been seen as important at the start of the relationship but can, in time, produce an irreconcilable rupture.

A further area of difficulty, one which is certainly not uncommon, relates to the different expectations men have of women, and women of men, as these often play a part in the ability of the pair to understand each other. Fortunately, there are signs in many young couples that the differences in this respect are lessening. As a generalization to which there are many exceptions, men are more comfortable showing their warmth and caring by actions, whereas women are more likely to express their feelings verbally. A woman might expect her partner to express his feelings in words but this expectation can undermine him and make him feel inadequate –

hardly a good basis for close communication unless the differences are acknowledged and accepted.

*Becoming Parents*
A number of marriages fail while the woman is pregnant or during the early months of the infant's life. This is a time of extra stress and fresh responsibilities, sometimes before the baby is born, which the husband may find too difficult to handle, especially if he feels marginalized or excluded from the new relationship. It is often the case that the birth of the first child is the largest change a marital relationship will experience, one which requires partners to make substantial adjustments in the way they see each other, and how each sees him- or herself. In addition to the positive feelings of pride and pleasure there can be negative ones of jealousy.

A small baby takes a great deal of time and energy; the unexpected tiredness is something impossible for parents to imagine in advance. Some fathers find their inability to help with a crying baby difficult to deal with. Painful feelings from childhood, perhaps of helplessness, are evoked to the extent that the solution is to leave the family. It is not surprising that this is a difficult time for many couples, especially those who lack support.

*Behaviour and Personality*
In some marriages one partner has finally given up hope that the other will change or relinquish unacceptable behaviour. 'I knew he drank before we were married but I didn't know he was so dependent on alcohol'; 'I knew she had a quick temper but I never expected to have to deal with such frequent bouts of uncontrolled anger.'

A spouse may leave the relationship because he or she finds the partner's mental state or paranoid personality too undermining to tolerate, especially if, in practice, the partner communicates by being critical, irresponsible, hostile or domineering. In these situations the children are doubly affected by having to deal with a difficult or unbalanced parent as well as losing the more stable one. Sometimes one of the children, quite often the oldest, can become burdened by the responsibility they have had to shoulder. A partner who is dependent on drugs or alcohol or who dominates the family by abusive acts can also be said to have a personality disorder and this is an important reason for the failure of a relationship.

A conventional reason for break-up, one that is indeed common though less so than is popularly supposed, is an unsatisfactory sexual relationship. Infidelity can be symptomatic of problems rather than the reason partners separate.

## Communicating

Ways of relating to each other also lie at the heart of many difficulties. For some people inadequate communication results from a failure to express positives, leaving the partner feeling undermined and valueless. For them intimacy gives the right to criticize. One damning statement implying a failure in communication is, 'I can read his [or her] mind. I know just what he is thinking.' This mind-reading is usually negative and by seeing situations in such a simple way results in a failure to check what the other person is really feeling.

A failure in communication causing an emotional gap between the partners may be a factor in the breakdown of a relationship although it is never the sole explanation for the difficulties. A husband who no longer loves his wife might 'stonewall' her by not looking at her, being distant and not listening when she tries to talk to him. His wife might have similar feelings but shows them through an attitude of disgust, and repeatedly complaining and criticizing him (Gottman 1991). In time the hurt and anger make a divide too wide to be closed. The couple stop giving each other any sense that they are valued by showing kindness, by consideration or by making positive comments. The marriage has lost warmth as well as any closeness and sharing, and before long there is no hope of improvement; it is time to get help – or separate.

One way of thinking about communication is to contrast an immature approach with a mature one. What distinguishes them, it has been postulated (Beal and Hochman 1991), hinges on whether a person is aware of the difference between fact and opinion. Immature people respond by not being able to consider the point of view of others or to make compromises; their feelings dominate. Arguments are resolved in three different ways: avoiding the real issues or not discussing them; adapting to them, which means that one partner has to suppress his or her feelings; or engaging in open conflict. As a result none of the differences is resolved and they are continually recycled.

In contrast, a mature solution focuses on reason, openness and trust. Mature people can accept changes and manage tension and have become emotionally freed from their family of origin so that unmet emotional needs from childhood no longer dominate, allowing reason to be exercised when necessary. Expressed more simply, the relationship starts with being 'in love'; that is, the partner is idealized, supplying unchallenged unmet emotional needs. This is wonderful but doesn't survive the stresses of living together and the anxieties present in most marriages. If the 'in love' changes to a more realistic loving then all will be well. Reality needs compromise, a lot of giving and some taking; it requires maturity and reasoning.

Communication takes many forms. There is no marriage without conflict, and coming to terms with conflict makes for growth and development (Pincus and Dare 1978). But it is a matter of degree. There are people for whom conflict has a positive connotation, people who cannot tolerate being ignored and people who enjoy the point-scoring. The rows help to establish identity – 'Nobody gets the better of me' – and may be a re-enactment of childhood sibling rivalry. Others say the rows are better than boredom. One wife described the exchanges she had with her partner as like a chess game of attack and counter-attack – and making up was worth the stress. This, of course, fails to take into consideration the children, who are not aware of the subtleties of the relationship, only of their fear that the situation might get out of control.

For some the break-up of the marital relationship is completely unexpected, like a thunderstorm on a fine day, as one child expressed it; another likened it to an electric shock. But, perhaps for the majority, angry feelings precede the break-up. Ending the rows is by far the most frequent reason children give when they think about the positives which have occurred following the separation, thus giving an important reason for addressing this pervasive problem. To do so could help to reduce the number of failed marriages; as could an attempt to understand why this destructive relationship occurs and what, if anything, could be done to stop it. But to make even a very small change in a relationship is very difficult, particularly because the other partner is likely to resist changes in any possible way.

Before any action can be taken there must be some important changes in thinking. The first is to accept that nobody is responsible for someone else's behaviour, nor can they do much to change it. To attempt to do so by criticism or fear might work in the short term but there will be untoward consequences. Women especially are conditioned to accept responsibility for the behaviour of other family members whereas in fact their responsibility is for their own thoughts and feelings, actions and reactions.

## Anger

What is the purpose of anger and does it achieve anything? It is not really about leaving coffee cups around or forgetting to buy the cat food; these are merely the beginning of another approaching storm, which ends either with more hurt feelings, or with making up, which can of course be a reason for the angry outburst. This will be the pattern until one of the partners, usually the one who minds most, deliberately addresses the underlying issues, a stressful operation which will in all probability require the help of a counsellor. It could mean having to consider how the reaction relates to past experience, particularly that of childhood. In addition, that person will have to look at his or her own contribution to what is happening, an exercise which is very different from taking the blame.

Another change in thinking is to accept that not to respond, even by doing nothing, has consequences. Any response gets another response, the pattern is circular. In contrast, offers to perform helpful though unwelcome actions if the other partner has a problem are not usually what is wanted; rather it is to give support. Such well-motivated intervention can lead the partner to feel grateful and at the same time resentful because dependence carried with it a message about an inability to cope.

Furthermore, excuses for anger are not valid. Nevertheless, the way the partner behaved or even how he or she looked can be an excuse to justify anger – 'He was being impossible.'; 'She deliberately broke the rules, she knows I can't stand it when she ....' Mary was almost permanently angry with her unemployed husband, Mike, who some-how always managed to find money for alcohol. Her anger had had no effect on him at all; his promises were soon broken and her anger continued to be the way she showed her concern for him. His drinking continued as an expression of his resentment at being dependent on her, something he could easily justify to himself – 'Anyone with a wife who carries on like she does needs to drown his sorrows.' Her nagging and worrying were to no avail; she was taking responsibility for both of them.

It is not capitulation to decide to give up a response which is not working, such as a martyred silence, threats, put-downs, nagging, revenge ('you did this, so I will do that') or making undefined complaints such as, 'you are always lazy/selfish/insensitive', which merely serves to let the offender off the hook – there is nothing he or she needs to do.

Mary's attempt to change her relationship with her drinking husband was not easy. She talked to him about her regret that she had fallen into the trap of nagging him all the time, almost like his mother had, and had lost sight of the capable strong man he once had been. In future she could respect his independence and not try to be responsible for both of them. For her to be a person in her own right, not 'Mike's wife', was hard, and he resisted the change strongly. There were many setbacks before they could reach a satisfactory relationship in which there was mutual respect and communication, one that included many positive caring comments. He was no longer fearful that he would lose his wife.

Situations may arise in which it does not seem possible to confront the person who caused the anger directly. Among them might be dealing with the impossible parent; or the difficult child who, it is thought, would be harmed by having limits set; or, outside the home, the unreasonable boss; or the missing car dealer who cheated you. In the first instance anger may not be given expression because of a more fundamental problem, the fear of being alone, and losing a close relationship; unexpressed anger has become so powerful it could destroy everything. At this point it is questionable whether it is worth maintaining the status quo.

Finally, and most painfully, there is the need to consider what the underlying reason for the anger is: does it relate to feeling worthless and undervalued? To being powerless without control? To being exploited or emotionally abused? Or feeling unloved and unwanted? Is there an expectation that the other partner can mind-read? Is there a better way of meeting these needs? Anger is part of being alive; it is an emotion like love, sadness or fear, and should not be denied or ignored but expressed in ways which are direct, rather than destructive.

**Some Reactions Following the Decision to Part**

For some partners the relationship has been too dire and relief is the overwhelming reaction to the separation. Others find that breaking the bonds which have lasted years means that what has been built up is shattered, and the familiar, even if it is not what is wanted, is missed. Feelings which are more akin to grieving after a bereavement are not uncommon even for those who welcomed the separation.

Not infrequently, one or both parents go through phases. They may find it difficult to believe they are being abandoned and in consequence are likely to be engulfed by sadness, but also by anger. The despair and depression that normally accompany such feelings will have to be worked through before the next phase, that of acceptance, is reached. It is only then that the future can be faced, one which will be very different from that imagined before but for which every ounce of courage is likely to be needed to cope with the responsibilities alone and eventually to find fulfilment and happiness. This task is made more difficult because of the lack of any ritual ending to a failed marriage. As a result the responses of friends and relations vary, in contrast with the general reaction of sadness and sympathy following separation because of death. It is a long process, but one made easier if there are understanding people around.

Lessons might be learnt from other countries. It has been claimed in an Australian magazine article, for instance, that nineteen out of twenty divorces are settled amicably (*New Women*, July 1998). In that article six rules are suggested for parents whose relationship has failed. Although five of these do not focus on the children, the sixth acknowledges that there could be difficulties over contact with them.

- Don't blame everything on your partner and remember the positives in the marriage.

- Keeping talking to each other; not lies, but talk about real issues.

- Don't be emotional when you should be legal. Counselling is to help see things from a different point of view; avoid hurt and anger getting in the way.

- Counselling may not be the best solution but could be the one you can live with.

- Be reasonable, use self-control so you do not react to every little thing. The goal should be that you have NOT acted unreasonably over any situation at any point.

- Be generous over contact, and do your best to maintain positive relationships with the other parent. Being a co-parent will need some negotiation. One of the worst situations is if the wife doesn't want the children to see their father and he retaliates by using financial pressure.

It is worth bearing in mind these various reasons why marriages fail, though it is not the causes but the effects which are our real concern. It is relevant to understand parents' reactions at the time of separation because they have a close bearing on how the children feel about their situation and how they are likely to feel in the future.

The pressures and responsibility of marriage, and especially of parenthood, can prove to be just too much for some parents, causing them to opt out of the relationship. For them and others there is a strong argument for giving more support and thought to preventing the break-up of the relationship at a much earlier stage, and it is much more important to do so if they have children. To concentrate on the procedures for obtaining a divorce can give the impression that there is an expectation that marriages are likely to fail – but nobody said changing public opinion was easy.

# 2    At the Time of Separation

## Some Difficulties Parents May Encounter

Society seems to expect divorce to have terrible consequences for the children, but the common assumption that this is inevitable is questionable. A good outcome depends to a considerable extent on the quality of the parental relationship following separation. Parents able to recover reasonably quickly, putting aside any feelings of anger and hurt caused by the separation so that they do not become pervasive, can then put their children's needs first, and by doing so, are making an important contribution to their well-being. Those parents who still have respect for each other and can be civil, or even friendly, in addition to sharing concern about their children, are doing the best they can at a difficult time.

Both parents may want divorce or separation because they believe their relationship has finally ended. But among the many whose marriage is finished, it is often the case that one partner does not want to separate and has had to accept the situation unwillingly. For that partner, feelings of hurt and betrayal lead to sadness and regret, displays of anger and sometimes uncharacteristic spite, all of which are difficult to control. Children rarely appreciate that these are basically common, even normal, reactions to grieving. All they see is an unhappy, angry parent and, because they are children, can blame themselves for causing such unhappiness.

Lone parents, besides feeling anxious about their often broken-hearted children who might be blaming them for the break-up and rejecting them for not keeping the marriage together, are likely to be worried about how they will manage to survive given new pressures such as complicated finances and unfamiliar household tasks. Should they try to find a job and would the cost of a child-minder be prohibitive, or are they better off on welfare benefit until the children are older? Nothing appears clear-cut; there are no obvious answers.

There are other worries, too: meetings with solicitors, court appearances and problems associated with having to be rehoused may have to be faced, and the stress of arranging contact can be as big a worry as having little money. More than one lone parent has said that the thing she dreads most is a solicitor's letter arriving on the mat. It is no wonder that this is perhaps the most stressful time in their lives, a time when their normal level of childcare and understanding is lower than usual. They are emotionally drained by this monumental load, to which might be added guilt, because they know it is near-impossible to meet the emotional needs of the children at a time when they are obsessed with their own feelings.

## Involving the Children

Many children have a two-fold wish: that their parents should live together so they are an intact family again, and that they will love each other. It is when they have, with difficulty, faced the second of these and know that it will never happen, that they can accept reality and begin to see things in a different light. For those children whose feelings have not been appreciated at the time, who have not been helped to come to terms with the separation or were not told about what was happening, their fantasy of the parents living together again can transcend their remarriage and last into adulthood. One thirty-year-old man, when talking about his parents' divorce twenty years previously, wept. The trauma, or for him the tragedy, happened yesterday.

On their part, parents are commonly concerned as to whether they should hide their distress from the children to avoid upsetting them more than necessary. The answer to this kind of question depends greatly on the long-term relationship between parent and child, but it is likely that the children are upset themselves and that if Mum cries in secret then they also keep their sorrow hidden; by so doing they have to hide their wish to be comforted.

However much parents want to avoid upsetting the children, they have to tell them that they are going to separate, or to reveal that one parent has already left the family home for good, and this can be an immensely painful undertaking, stemming in part from their own mixed feelings. They also know that their children are almost inevitably going to be upset and that they themselves are likely to inflict distress and anxiety on to them. It can be the finality which is difficult, especially if there have been previous separations. Is this the time when it really will be for good? No less hard is the situation where the separation is final but the non-resident parent is having difficulty leaving, saying that it is best for the children if he returns home each weekend. It may be best for him but the children can be confused by the two messages they are receiving, even though it is important that he sees them often at this time.

One child of divorced parents, now a young adult, has a close relationship with both her parents. The separation took place when she was six, many years before, and as she talked about this, remarked that she had always felt very protective towards her father, and still did. Saying this led her to wonder where the feeling came from, as it was obvious to everyone that her father was perfectly capable of looking after himself. She then remembered the time when the children were told about the impending separation; all the family, parents and children were crying, but it was her father's tears which moved her and had remained with her into adulthood. The telling can have long-term consequences, as it did for this well-adjusted young adult.

*Telling the Children – Two Examples*
The three children were playing with Lego in the hall; mum and dad were arguing upstairs and although the children were aware of the noise and were always anxious at these times, it was a familiar situation. But when their dad suddenly stormed downstairs, his face contorted with rage, their anxiety turned to fear. 'That's it,' he said to the children, 'I'm off and from now on your mother can look after you.' The door shuddered as he slammed it, leaving three children looking at each other in horror; the worst had happened. They did not see their father for three months and at no time were they given any explanation. They were too scared to ask their mum questions because she was so distraught that in their eyes she seemed like a stranger, and they were afraid of the answers they might receive.

They showed their distress in a variety of ways but the main effect on all of them was a loss of confidence which affected many aspects of their lives. Kim, the three-year-old, believed Daddy had left because she was naughty; last night when he told her to go to bed she had said, 'No, no, no I won't' and made him cross; obviously it was her fault. She thought one day Daddy would come back, but meanwhile she was secretly anxious that Mummy might leave too and then there would be nobody to look after her. No wonder she was having bad dreams and clinging to her mother.

Her six-year-old brother Mike was openly sad, preoccupied with his longing for Daddy to return. His mind was full of terrifying fantasies of being abandoned, unsafe and alone. Teachers at school were angry with him because he was restless and noisy and unable to keep still, but in a sort of way he found this reassuring – at least he was getting a reaction. Sometimes he had bouts of uncontrollable anger but some nights in bed he would put his head under the pillows and sob as if his heart would break wondering if, as he hadn't been told anything, Daddy had died. His school behaviour presented what the teachers found a contradiction; with the children he often seemed happy enough, joining in the normal rowdy play of six-year-olds, but progress with his studies was giving cause for concern. It was a demonstration of the often unrecognized fact that children express their grieving in a different way from adults.

Richard, his nine-year-old brother, was in trouble; this usually kind child was bullying and breaking his most treasured toys and had been stealing small things from other children at school. However, inside his head he felt he was being pulled in two, trying to reconcile his love and longing for his dad with his anger, because his dad had left the family and made everyone unhappy. Richard could also have had a vague hope that his parents might unite in concern over the things he was doing, because he was hiding his distress behind a smokescreen of anger.

Because of her own pain, their mother was unable to tell them what was happening or to discuss the possible changes in their lives in the future. The important question they wanted answered was whether they would see Dad again, and if so, how soon. Fortunately, once these parents, who were caring when not preoccupied with their own problems, had become calmer they appreciated that mistakes had been made and were able to respond to their children's needs, thus avoiding the risk of inflicting any long-term emotional harm. The children learned that nothing is wholly bad, even when parents have separated, and that there are always some gains, however small.

In another instance, parents of two children had planned what they could say. Early one evening the mother of Mark and Laura, aged six and eight, said to them, 'When the programme has finished, Dad and I need to talk to you.' They were rather apprehensive because Mum and Dad looked so grim. Then Dad explained that a long time ago he and Mum loved each other and decided they wanted to get married and live together. There were lots of good things about this, especially having children, but over time there were lots of problems and neither of them was happy. They tried to make things right again and they talked to people whose job it was to help, but nothing was successful. As a result they have decided that it would be better for them to live separately. Mum and the children would stay here, in their present house, and Dad would move out.

The children listened in silence; then Dad continued, telling them that the important thing for them was to know that even though he would be living in a different house they would see him as often as possible, at least every week. This they received with relief and they were pleased to hear him say that he would still be concerned about them and their lives, as well as what was happening at school, and he would ring them up besides seeing them. Perhaps things weren't going to be as awful as they first thought they might be.

Mum told them that loving between grown-ups was different from loving children; although they had stopped loving each other, they could never stop loving their own children. They said that being parents was different from being married; for Mark and Laura, they would be their parents for ever. Dad reinforced the message, repeating that although he and Mum would be in different places they would still be their parents and the love and care from both of them would continue as it always had.

The children asked other questions about what would happen. Some of them the parents couldn't answer, so they responded in the way most helpful to the children, explaining they didn't know but would tell them as soon as possible. Among the many other questions they wanted to know was whose fault it was. Was it theirs? This was the first of many times they wanted to hear it said that their parents got married before there were any children, and to end the marriage was also not about children. And it was a tremendous relief to hear Mum say she would never never leave them whatever happened.

The children were distressed, but not devastated. They were pleased that both parents were concerned about them and comforted by the thought that they would continue to still have both parents, not one. They were also quite relieved that the arguments, which had become very worrying recently, would stop. They knew that they could ask more questions when they were ready. Even so, the children were sad and cried a lot, and were also angry, a feeling expressed by their changed behaviour for a short while. Nevertheless, they derived some comfort from knowing that Mum and Dad would help them with this unwelcome change in their lives. They still had two parents and were special to both of them; they would be OK.

## What do Children Understand?

It is not always easy for adults to appreciate the limits of children's understanding. An unexpected instance in a quite different setting illustrates this. While I was visiting a hospital in Washington DC a play leader explained to a seven-year-old who had approached us, that I came from England and spoke differently from how they did. His eyes widened with wonder and, after a pause, he asked me how I spoke if I didn't use my mouth. Children of this age can be equally confused by 'divorce', 'contact', 'parental responsibility' and other words and phrases which they hear adults use, sometimes because of their literal acceptance of the words. Children's understanding depends in part on their age and maturity and what they can properly be expected to grasp, and in part on their long-term relationship with both parents and the level of trust they have in them both.

Adults have to take the major decisions but they are more able to make the best arrangements if they know what each child in the family feels and they listen closely to their opinions. Younger ones want to know just what divorce means and why it is happening in their family. The children know of other families where adults quarrel but stay together. How could their parents choose not to stay together? 'Mummy and Daddy love you but don't love each other' is not satisfactory for children who, until that moment, believed that love was for ever. If, when you get angry with someone and stop loving him or her, they go away, then your other parent could also leave you. This is a perfectly logical and frequently felt worry that needs to be addressed openly and fairly early.

When the children are told about the separation can be important. Charlotte, a ten-year-old, was told by her mother in the car on the way to school, leaving her daughter to survive a day she thought she would remember all her life. Nor is it a good time when there are exams to worry about. Most children remember how and when they were told many years afterwards, because for many of them it was the biggest trauma they had ever experienced. For those parents who are unable to co-operate to the extent that they cannot put the feelings of children first, the next best solution might be for both to tell the children separately and as nearly as possible after the event.

However they are told, children are likely to be upset and time is needed for them to heal. Sympathetic telling will not take away their fundamental feeling of sadness but it can avoid the children being left with a long-term loss of confidence arising from the feeling that they don't matter.

## Separation or Intact-but-Hostile Family?

For the child the main gain from the separation may be that the hostility between parents diminishes or even ends completely, though unfortunately the opposite may be true, for in not a few instances antagonism increases at the time of separation. However, for most children there is a more peaceful environment and the scars resulting from parental antagonism can begin to heal. This is not to say that tension from the unresolved problems may not continue; the uncertainty of the outcome remains, usually for months and probably longer. And if the family house has to be sold at such an emotional time, it will certainly add to the difficulties for parents and children alike.

When children whose parents have separated following a hostile relationship are asked if it would be better for them if their parents had stayed together, they invariably say it would be. For them the rows are familiar, they have learnt to deal with the antagonism and know strategies which help them cope with what for them is a part of their life. They hear but do not hear the angry words from downstairs, they are alert and ready to charge down the stairs if they think the violence is getting out of hand, or they relive their nightly fear that Dad will come home drunk again or Mum will make the house rattle as she slams the front door on her way out. It is all very familiar, but suppose this time she doesn't come home? They cannot fail to have some level of anxiety but see their family as no better, or worse, than the families of most of their friends. As one child said, 'Happy marriages belong in books.'

## Children's Questions

Many children express a great deal of anxiety about both their parents very soon after they have separated. Until parents have started on the road to recovery the children's questions can be painful – and possibly embarrassing for the parents to answer. It can be easier to cope with unreasonable behaviour than to be confronted directly with what gives rise to it.

They will want to know about things relating to the past: why it happened, who was to blame? Guilt is a feeling behind many of their questions in these early days. They desperately want to help but don't know what they could have done to stop it happening. Questions relating to the present are likely to be based on whether they will see the other parent, and if so, when and how often. They are worried about whether either of them is lonely or unhappy, for instance, and how they can possibly manage without the other. This concern is difficult for parents to appreciate because the children's own sadness and worry make them easily upset, quick to anger and generally unreasonable. Younger children may be further confused because they are unable to understand the meaning of 'next Saturday', much less 'for ever'.

And there will be questions about the future, including practical matters such as how poor the family will be, and whether they will have to live in a different house or go to a different school. But these are comparatively easy questions compared with the ones which reveal caring feelings for someone the resident parent may feel is the worst person in the world. However difficult it is for her mother, it not helpful for a child to know that questions about the absent parent are banned. One boy was told by his mother: 'I don't want to hear his name again in this house.' A girl was hit by her father every time she said something about Mummy to him. Restrictions of this kind are an added strain for an already vulnerable child. It is far better to answer questions about matters which involve children honestly, though not to share intimate details regarding the behaviour of the other parent which are not the concern of children. If circumstances make it impossible to give a straight answer, it will probably be more helpful to respond as Mark and Laura's parents did by saying that they will be told as soon as possible.

## Children's Worries

### Rejection

A common cause of worry for children is how Dad's or Mum's new partner will get on with them – and how they will get on with the new person. Although many children want Mum to have a new partner because they feel the family is not complete, or that a man around will help them feel safer, at the same time they are worried about the situation. Suppose they will not be wanted, or the new boyfriend doesn't like them or has his own children? And if Daddy has a new girlfriend, she might have her own children; then they, his own children, could feel unwanted in either home. Even if it is true that they will continue to be loved whoever joins the family unit, and this is clearly expressed by both parents, words alone, without actions, are not enough to allay their fears of rejection.

They want to know that although they will live with one parent they will see the other as often as possible and both parents want this to happen. This proviso is important because it reduces the risk of the child feeling disloyal. It is a sad fact that in some families this is not always the case and in these circumstances it is kinder to explain the true situation to children in the most sensitive and supportive way, rather then leaving them for years with a hope that will not be realized.

### Contact Arrangements

Children, like parents, want to sort out some of the minor details which arise and may cause difficulties. Will toys be taken from one house to another or stay in one house? Will Dad be able to come into the house or will he leave them at the gate? Who will help with weekend homework? If the battles continue, can they agree to go to school functions on different nights? What will happen if it's Dad's weekend and they've been invited to a party? These are the sort of small points that can inflame a volatile situation.

*Worry about Loyalty*
Another and more important source of stress relates to how parents use the children to further their own ends, a situation discussed more fully in later chapters; but it would help if, at the time of divorce, children heard parents say that they will not use them as messengers and will not ask what the other parent has been doing. Children should also be made aware that one parent will do his or her best not to say bad things about the other, though sometimes they might forget and need reminding – or forgiving.

*Worries about Being Different*
Children's loss of self-confidence, something which is temporary for many, is fairly general, and the sense of shame that causes or contributes heavily to it arises from the mistaken belief that they are the only one in their class whose parents do not live together. This, despite the fact that one in three will experience the divorce of their parents before they are sixteen. Parents, especially fathers, can do a great deal to counter their lowered self-esteem. Some are helped by talking to other children with separated parents or to caring adults outside the immediate family.

**The Importance of the Familiar**

Because of all the changes which are inevitable with divorce, as well as some that are likely at this time, the more familiar things children can retain in their lives, the better. Contact with relatives can be very important, especially where the relationship with them is close; parents of the non-resident parent are often very special for children and adult antagonism shouldn't deprive them of a loving relationship. To do so can confirm for the child the feeling of being abandoned because she is horrible. Familiar activities and rituals can play an important part in a child's efforts to survive this trauma.

*Moving House*
For many children, a great source of worry is that they might have to move to a new house, one which is likely to be smaller and less convenient. This could mean that they may have to change to a new school, perhaps in a different kind of neighbourhood, a change which will make the separation public knowledge before they are ready to

share what some see as private. The result could be a loss of friends and leisure activities in the old neighbourhood, with perhaps some difficulty in replacing both. To have a parent leave, and then to forfeit the image of an intact family is one thing; to have to give up a home, for some, can be almost as terrible.

### Siblings

Brothers and sisters can also be very important for children; as one child said recently, 'Unless their parents have divorced, other children have no idea at all what it is like. No idea at all.' Even though to the outsider the sibling relationship might seem to be one of antagonism, a brother or sister does know what it is like and, without their putting the feeling into words, the children are often very dependent on each other.

In some countries it is usual, in the interests of fairness to the parents, to split the children – one living with Dad, one with Mum – but the arrangements can entail difficulties for the parents and be far from satisfactory for the children. In every instance where this is proposed a great deal of thought should be given to it, and it should be fully discussed with the children to avoid either of them feeling rejected, before any decision is made. Because they can rely on each other in a very different way from their relationship with other people, adults may only be aware of the rivalry between them. Less obvious is how they are important to each other and give support in quite subtle ways, and at a time of change they are very much a part of what is familiar.

# 3 Children's Reactions: Behaviour

How do children experience divorce? What are the strategies they use for dealing with what can be the trauma of separating parents and what feelings might result? This and the following chapter are based primarily on the experience of listening to children but the observations are, of necessity, general, because separation is not one event but has a history which every family member has been part of and contributed to.

As has been said before, divorce or separation need not always be devastating for children. Certainly this is what many children come to realize when hostility between parents diminishes, especially if they have been involved in the antagonism. But they can be helped to think differently about the events. At the outset they have to accept that the separation is an adult problem, that the adults are responsible people and have to be trusted to sort out those matters which belong to their relationship. Many children voice their despair and guilt at not being able to unite their parents; children have become a part of the problem but are greatly troubled because they cannot find a way of helping to find a solution, which of course cannot or should not be their responsibility.

Most children, when their parents separate, experience such complex and changeable emotions that it is difficult for adults to understand them. Today they are racing around shouting with their friends with obvious enjoyment but within a short time they are weeping and overwhelmed with sadness. Before long there is another change; they are defiant and difficult. Parents, whose own feelings are also mixed, are confused by this chameleon in the house. Has she got over it, or not?' What can they do to help? Nothing seems right.

At the time when their parents separate children are likely to have conflicting reactions and most will recover, but it will take some time and it cannot be presumed that silence means the child has 'got over it'. Ewen was thought to have taken the separation of his parents very well, until his dog died nine months later – then he sobbed as if his heart would break. By then he was able bring his pent-up grief into the open. A number of reasons might account for his behaviour; it could have been too difficult to deal with the divided loyalty, his sadness at the time was too great or with all the emotions in the family he had little hope of being comforted; it did not signify that the experience was not important but that he, as do many children, had responded very much later, triggered by what was for Ewen another tragedy.

## Reactions Within the Family

Amongst the many factors influencing children's reactions to separation are those which can be related to their personality. Some are resilient, with good coping strategies; they are skilled at finding supportive people although they are usually of an independent frame of mind. They are likely to manage well, but also can be clever at hiding their feelings, especially if they are concerned to protect others in the family. At the opposite pole from them are the children who lose all confidence and see the situation as being unfair; they feel rejected and full of despair. They are very obviously desperately unhappy.

### Why Boys and Girls React Differently

Frequently, boys are thought to have more difficulty when parents separate than girls, though this can change at adolescence when girls quite often demonstrate emotional problems (Wallerstein 1988, Hetherington 1989). Other research finds this not proven (Rodgers and Pryor 1998). The statement is very much a generalization – some boys are exceptionally sensitive as some of their comments recorded in this book demonstrate. For others their difficulties may not be primarily related to the separation but to their resident parent being their mother, especially if they are living in an all-female household. Nearly half of all fathers sever the connection with their sons soon after the divorce is finalized, often leaving their son without a role model unless a new partner joins the family. The boy's attempt to establish or express his masculinity is interpreted as aggressive behaviour; but then his distress at losing his father cannot be expressed openly – boys don't cry, do they? If his identity as a male is not respected it makes it almost impossible for him to respect himself.

Sadly for most, the situation is not solved by living with a depressed father who might drink too much or is too angry or distraught to help his son with growing up, a situation confirmed by ChildLine (1998) who found that proportionally more boys who live with their fathers ring them, compared with those who live with their mothers. Many fathers have difficulty showing closeness and understanding, many are working long hours and expect their children to cook the meals and clean the house and those who have been left may talk in angry terms about their ex-wife, who is loved and missed by her son. Many do not give their sons support or enjoy them and help them to develop confidence in a way no one else can. Perhaps if more fathers appreciated the importance of having a warm relationship with their sons, and daughters, and they appreciated how important they are for their child's development, boys especially would not be so harmed by divorcing parents.

Girls are in a slightly easier position because they are likely to be living with their role model, their mother, and they are more likely to receive a sympathetic response when they are distressed.

*Indifference?*
By behaving with apparent indifference – and this is not uncommon – a child may be following a family pattern. Except for his outbursts of anger from time to time, Neil's father was a man who showed very little outward sign of emotion, whether pleasure or warmth, anxiety or concern. Neil's mother, also fairly unemotional and restrained, felt too inhibited by her husband to show her feelings. It was not surprising that Neil, an only, lonely child, modelled himself on his father and also lacked spontaneity; he continued to play with his computer when his mother told him his father was leaving. It may be that unless something happens to change this pattern of behaviour, from an unusual denial of feelings to a more outgoing one, this ten-year-old, with very few social skills, could have problems with relationships in the future.

When his parents separated, another boy, twelve-year-old Jamie, was too overcome with sadness and anger to risk expressing any feelings. He feigned indifference and behaved as if nothing had happened. If anyone tried to talk to him he became abusive and appeared to have no interest in what had happened. 'It's nothing to do with me', he said. Even when it was found that he had been playing truant from school for weeks his behaviour was not linked by teachers to the fact that his parents were living apart, nor did the parents themselves guess the cause of Jamie's trouble. Fortunately an understanding GP referred him to a Child and Family Clinic where he felt safe enough to express some of his sadness at what had happened, and to talk about his belief that his parents had betrayed him. What they had seen as his maturity had deceived them and reinforced their hope that he wasn't suffering any ill effects from their separation.

These boys (they are usually boys) might be the sort of children who never involve themselves in adult concerns; perhaps they are obsessed with their computer or playing football, and their indifference can easily be considered an indication of emotional immaturity. The reasons, though, might be very different. For some of them the adult world and its problems are not interesting or may be too complex for them to understand, especially if they have been told repeatedly, over many years and about many different topics, that they are too young to understand what adults are talking about.

Apparent indifference on the part of the child may mask deep unhappiness and distress, arising from an inability to express feelings, perhaps because they are afraid of losing control. 'If I started to cry I would never stop', said one teenage boy. Children like this may belong to a family which does not consider it appropriate to show feelings of distress – or in some families, any feelings at all – or possibly another family member is so emotional they feel there is no room for their distress; and anyway, if they did express it the exposure would be greeted with derision, the last response they want. In family life a variety of situations make it unsafe or at least difficult for children to express feelings which might make other people uncomfortable.

In those families where the father is physically violent to the mother or to them, the children may want the family to break up, but often, what an outsider sees as an intolerable situation, children wish to continue. In their view the unknown alternative could easily be worse; they might have to 'go into care', which is an adult threat, and not see their parents. In the worst case Dad could be put in prison and it would be their fault. And although Dad or Mum behaves badly, they are their parents and despite all the other feelings they have, most children, but again not all, still love both parents. Most take the view that it is better to leave things as they are.

Unhappy, intact families can be unhappy in secret. By separating, parents have made what the children usually see as a private matter into a public affair and, as a result, they come to feel they are different and inferior; parents' failure can be felt by children as their failure too. Perhaps at school they give a message of being vulnerable and in consequence may be being taunted or bullied, though some of these children do the bullying.

However, if subsequently the separation proves to be reasonably harmonious, they modify their view, especially if the marital hostility ends and the children do not lose touch with their father, which is what most fear. The change usually means less money or even poverty for the children, which causes a great deal of stress; but this can be countered in some respects by their being aware that living separately helps both their parents to be happier. Mostly the children who do not want to continue the relationship with their father are those who are frightened of him.

### Children's Role in the Family
Children's reactions will differ quite widely according to the particular roles they give themselves in the family; each one will have individual

feelings and it cannot be assumed that the most outgoing one is speaking for all. Almost from the start, some children have personalities which cause them to be interested in other people. They want to know what adults are doing and where they are going, and as they grow up they become conscious of adult feelings and relationships. They know when it is time to stop doing what is not approved of to avoid trouble. Their antennae are picking up vibes, questioning, wondering. Others are more self-contained and able to amuse themselves for a long time. They are in their own world of imagination, solving problems or finding out about things rather than people; for them the concerns of adults are too difficult or not interesting. In the context of divorce the first group of children will probably want more details and answers to more questions than those who can escape into their own pursuits; each group will have different reactions and different ways of expressing feelings.

The child's position in the family can also affect her reaction. Quite often one child, maybe the eldest or the only girl, is the one who is more involved, more worried or burdened with the responsibility of having parents who separate. She can be the confidante for a parent, or the peacemaker. She may feel, with the welter of emotions around, that she alone is the repository for the sadness in the family. Other children, because of their personality or individual relationship with each parent, allot themselves different tasks: one may worry about Dad, anxious about whether he can take care of himself or whether he will be lonely; another may be the one who is angry on behalf of the others. 'How could our parents do this to us when they say they love us? They had a choice.'

*Loyalty*
A very general problem for children is how to remain loyal to both parents; some find it too difficult and respond by aligning with only one. When this problem occurs the child's mental energy is devoted to concern and anxiety about a parent who might be either the resident or the non-resident one. This can be a situation with some emotional dangers, especially if the child takes the role of a substitute partner or is in a position of parenting his parent, because in these circumstances what is a healthy concern has resulted in crossing a generation boundary. 'You are the man of the house now' can be a tremendous responsibility for a ten-year-old who has more than enough anxieties of his own to deal with without taking on such an inappropriate load. Other children take over parenting their younger siblings, and this is a responsibility which, if it continues, sometimes helps their self-esteem but can also lead to resentment.

Some can find the problem of remaining loyal to both too difficult. 'I'm like a tennis ball', said one child, 'I'm batted between Mum and Dad all the time.' This is especially so if the beginnings and endings of contact visits are stressful. It is easier to be firmly on the side of one parent in order to avoid this chasm but this option does not necessarily mean the child is not desperate to see Dad; rather it is the case that she cannot see a way of doing so without dire consequences.

*Pre-Separation Fears*
A child who is indicating stress openly by crying, or indirectly by behaving in an unacceptable way or showing physical symptoms, is usually assumed to be worried about missing an absent parent. This can be so, but sometimes the separation is a catalyst making possible the expression of long-term bottled-up emotions which are related to stress in his early and subsequent history, or to living in a household where the two people who matter most to him have been verbally or physically hostile to each other for a long time. In such circumstances the child has lived in fear and with the anxiety or even expectation that someone will be harmed, or leave. Such a situation cannot fail to affect him in varying degree. The tears may indeed be of sadness, but also, in part, of relief. 'Were there any concerns about the child before the separation?' 'What was the atmosphere like in the family before?' These could be relevant questions but they are not usually asked by those concerned to help.

**Children's Strategies**

Children develop a variety of strategies to help them deal with a situation which they do not want and is not of their making. Some of these responses may be interpreted by adults as naughty, spiteful or aggressive, or harmful to the children themselves or others. It can take quite a lot of understanding by parents, who are dealing with an experience which has been a painful one for them, to link such behaviour to the child's feelings about the separation.

Frequently children suffering from loss have psychosomatic symptoms such as pains, sleep disruption or skin rashes. They may bite and kick or develop eating disorders. Some don't want to eat; others can't stop. Eleven-year-old Hannah was in some danger of becoming anorexic until her anxiety was understood. She had been 'Daddy's girl' but she feared her absent father could reject her if she grew up. To avoid this and stay as his little girl led to her not wanting to eat. In contrast, boys are more likely to find an outward expression of their grief and anxiety and may become highly active or difficult to control, refusing to do as they are told or to co-operate. 'I can't make Dad come home but I can make other people unhappy too and at least they won't forget I'm around.'

If their distress is dealt with sympathetically and they find acceptable ways of putting their feelings outside themselves, after a while they recover well. If, on the other hand, they can find no satisfactory form of expression they may resort to hurting themselves or others or find other detrimental solutions.

Anticipating bad consequences is another strategy, one that is adopted in the expectation that the loss will be repeated. To pre-empt might be a protection against serious loss. 'I knew this would happen. I always miss out and things always go wrong for me.' Others are afraid to take risks and avoid close relationships because of the expectation they will get hurt by a further loss. This can lead to the belief that you aren't entitled to good things and if by chance they come your way somehow you make sure loss will follow; it becomes a self-fulfilling prophecy. Others react by always expecting perfect relationships, fastening on the smallest sign which can be interpreted negatively. They cannot accept that it is normal for everyone, adult and child, to have good days and bad days and that the bad days don't mean failure and disastrous consequences.

## Reactions at Different Ages

When thinking about how children of various ages react, the emphasis has naturally to be on the differences, but it ought to be remembered that the similarities are greater than the differences. Many feelings are shared: it is their expression that differs. A sad preschool child might stop developing, become uninterested in playing and have problems in sorting out fantasy from reality; a sad ten-year-old boy might hide his sadness with anger, while a girl of the same age might express her feeling by crying in her bedroom for long periods; sad teenagers might worry about themselves in the future or might find concentration at school very difficult; all share the common emotion of sadness.

To decide whether one of these ages is worse for a child than another is not particularly important because the answer must depend in part on whether the short-term or long-term consequences are being considered and what the child's subsequent experiences have been. Research in America confirmed this view from a different standpoint: it was found that the more sophisticated the study, the smaller the effects; other variables including race, gender and class might have more influence (Amato and Keith 1991).

*Preschool Children*
Those under five are often thought to be especially vulnerable (Dominian et al. 1991 p. 29), a view upheld in America by a national survey involving 1,197 children (Elliott and Richards 1991). Three high-risk groups – adolescents, those experiencing a second divorce of their parents and very young children – have been identified by another American writer, who comments that the last group represents an entirely unexamined section of children (Wallerstein 1988). Ten years on this is still true, and among the very young it is the child whose main carer has left – the one to whom he is most closely attached, leaving him feeling abandoned – who is likely to be most at risk of long-term effects.

A third of children of divorced parents are under five and at present this large group receives very little help. Babies as young as seven or eight months will laugh when their parents are having fun, so it is reasonable to expect that they will also respond with sadness and anxiety to adults whose relationship is hostile. They could show their distress by crying, and by signs of fear at raised voices and angry distorted faces; or in a more general way, by being irritable and not sleeping. Their security is threatened. Those who are a year or two older might have their reactions overlooked, in part because they lack verbal skills to explain how confused or upset they are.

Young children believe they are the centre of the universe. They make things happen and if these are bad things then it is their fault. 'Daddy left because I spilt my orange juice.' 'Mummy and Daddy quarrelled because I made a fuss about going to bed.' They have difficulty in understanding concepts and their sense of time is not developed, so 'You will see Daddy at the week-end' has little meaning for them. In addition, they might believe that parents understand what they are feeling and must therefore know the terrible, angry, revengeful thoughts they have in their head. This makes them anxious on that score too.

Other worries relate to the thought that 'If Daddy has left, Mummy can too, and then who will get my dinner?' Such anxiety can lead to excessive clinging or a return to a phase of behaviour that has passed. They lose the ability to play creatively and often return to a past phase of development, a retreat into a time when life was more straightforward and understandable. Their coping mechanisms can include eating problems and excessive clinging.

Three-year-olds may have particular difficulties because of the phase of development they have reached. The little boy was just at the stage of 'joining the men', wanting Daddy to do things for him. He is going to be like daddy when he grows up but his model and the best person in the world didn't want him and has left him. He does not know why but his belief in magic is still intact. 'If I clean my teeth every night, wherever he is, Daddy will know and will come home again.' If he saw his father as a rival for his mother's affections, it is especially important for him to continue seeing his dad, otherwise he might believe that he is all-powerful and has driven Daddy away. Not surprisingly, monsters and vicious animals can invade his dreams, only for him they are not dreams. No wonder he is clinging and fearful in the daytime, miserable and whiny; no wonder he grieves with such intensity for his dad.

The three-year-old girl was going to marry Daddy when she grew up but now he has gone. She did not know why? Again, contact and reassurance are vital for the future image of such little girls. If he will come back she will never never do anything naughty again. Children of this age may be too young to understand what divorce means, but are not too young to feel lonely or abandoned. Four- and five-year-olds might stop speaking or revert to baby talk, or develop fears (especially at night) and wet their beds: expressed by the child psychologist Mildred Creak in an apposite phrase many years ago, they 'cry with their bladder'. For these children their belief is that Dad left them, not Mummy or anyone else.

The reason why Ivan, aged four, started to wet his bed after being dry for more than a year was very different and was related to contact visits after his dad had left; he was having to keep a secret. His paternal aunt, who was always present when he saw his father, told him that she was his real mummy and one day he would live with her but he must not tell the secret to his mother. This love expressed in such a harmful way was causing Ivan nightmares and led to his symptom. For a young child, not mature enough to understand, to be told that he must not tell a parent anything, especially if it concerns themselves, is usually tantamount to emotional abuse because of the tremendous mental strain it imposes; it runs contrary to the child's natural desire to share.

Other children who are subjected to similar insuperable dilemmas may display behaviour which is more appropriate for younger children; unable to move forward, they have become emotionally 'stuck' by fear. One little girl, also aged four, stopped talking completely; it was some time before the full extent of the abuse she had been subjected to was made known. She had lost trust in all adults and it was too dangerous for her to say anything at all.

Young children cannot understand properly what has happened in a divorce situation, still less why. Nor do they have the words to express the complexity of their feelings about it. They resort to demonstrating their emotions by their behaviour as well as in direct ways, such as crying. If you, the child, feel your distress is unnoticed because your parents are too busy with their own feelings, which are often quite different from yours, it is easier to get a reaction by making someone angry than by asking for what you really want, whether it is reassurance, an answer to a worrying question, or a hug.

Some of their difficulties are influenced by living in a discordant environment, one in which hostility is dominant. Eve, an intelligent little girl, was such a child. She lived in a fairly affluent family with her mother and father and her brother, who was two years older. From when she was a baby her mother, who had a strong identification with her daughter, had given a subtle message of approval when Eve had asserted herself and while she was still a toddler aggression towards other children was rewarded by attention ending in a hug. Eve's father disapproved but found the escalating rows with his wife too unbearable and so chose to accept the situation. In this family the key relationship was that between mother and daughter. Eve learnt that to 'stick up for herself' was approved behaviour; but her school was not so happy with this large, bright, bullying five-year-old who upset every child she encountered.

Predictably, by the age of seven, when her parents separated, she was showing highly disturbed behaviour. Her experience of a warm relationship had for many years been complicated by the approval of aggression and latterly by her own increasing awareness of the antagonism between her parents. It was not surprising that her self-esteem came from upsetting most children she encountered, especially the most vulnerable. The assumption that the divorce caused her problems – perfectly natural for anyone who didn't know the background – would be quite wrong.

*Middle Childhood*
The opinion that school children are more seriously affected than those of other ages is maintained by some. 'Several recent studies show that children from five to nine years are most affected by their parents' separation' (Wells 1993, p. 33). At this age the family is still central and parents are the best people in the world. For one to leave can shatter the child's security and cause tremendous grief.

Sophie's lone mother found it hard to understand her six-year-old daughter's plea for her to 'find a new daddy' when she knew how much

Sophie longed for her own father to return. Shopping trips became something of a nightmare for her mother. 'Look over there, he looks a kind man, why don't you marry him?' 'There's a very good-looking man who looks nice standing by his car. Please go and talk to him.' Sophie not only missed her dad but also missed belonging to what was for her a real family with a mum and a dad. Kevin, a child who had witnessed violence in his home and was very frightened of his dad expressed the same thought. 'Please find me a gentle dad', he said to his mum.

Slightly older boys tend to be noisy, active and perhaps defiant, all these reactions serving to hide their distress from being too oppressive and their excessive activity stopping them having to think the unthinkable – Dad has gone for ever. Understandably, these boys often have difficulty in sleeping and concentrating, which affects learning at school. Some over-eat or develop physical ailments. Many seven-year-olds also regress, for instance by thumb sucking, or they lose confidence in their ability to do simple tasks. 'It's boring', they say, which is more acceptable than 'I can't do it, it's too painful.' These are some of the ways children use to deal with the emptiness inside them though at times they can still sob with grief and long for the departed parent. Mostly these children live with their mother and some find that missing a male influence adds to the difficulties of adjusting to the changes.

Their understanding of permanence and their renunciation of magic, which at this age comes and goes, though it is never entirely lost, means that at times they believe Dad will return shortly, when he has done what he has to do, but at other times they are aware this is likely to be a permanent situation. Then they have, with reluctance, to change their perception of what has happened, a task sometimes accompanied by loneliness and fears of abandonment.

At around the age of eight, having made some big steps forward in maturity, boys especially have to face the fact that much of the time Dad is not around to give encouragement and approval or take part in activities with them. Stealing is a symptom frequently mentioned at this age, perhaps being an attempt to relieve the intense pain of loss which they carry inside them, while slightly older children sometimes hide their distress with anger; they bully and break, hit and hurt. This sort of behaviour is sometimes a child's attempt to give his mother a message that she can't cope with him so his father should come back. Other boys of this age may form a collusive relationship with their father whom they see as vulnerable, and they might have fantasies of effecting a reconciliation between the parents.

Some become the clown of the class. For a while the other children enjoy this, especially as someone else is getting into trouble, but soon they tire of it, leaving the 'clown', who is crying inside, even more bereft as he is called 'immature' and 'silly' by his peers. These children are not learning age-appropriate skills; they too have become 'stuck', though in a different way from the young children discussed above. They will have difficulty making friends because they don't know when to stop attracting attention and they are not picking up clues from other children about appropriate behaviour. Their actions may contain an element of wanting to be punished to assuage the guilt they feel, or because they need confirmation that Dad doesn't like them and therefore nobody else will. At this time their unhappiness knows no end.

Both boys and girls can find it difficult to concentrate at school because of their preoccupation with the stresses at home, thus compounding their sense of failure, but for others school is a place of safety where routines give security and they can distance themselves from home worries. Many find it difficult to talk to parents; one eleven-year-old boy explained that he couldn't tell his parents how he felt because they were too angry to listen. A number of eleven- and twelve-year-olds have explosive outbursts and become vulnerable to depression, while others feel intense anger at one or both parents for causing the divorce. They, like children of other ages, are mourning the loss of an intact family whose break-up they have been unable to prevent. Many are deeply worried about one or other parent but, because of the parent's own distress (which children often interpret as anger aimed at them), are reluctant to show their concern and warm feelings. When they do, parents are often surprised and pleased.

*Teenagers*
Adolescence is claimed by some to be the worst time, especially for girls. Children at this age are certainly a high-risk group. The feelings of each child change quite frequently at different times and on different days and, as they grow, their perception of what happened and why, changes too. These will relate in part to their understanding and involvement in the separation, and in part to how other people who are important to them reacted at the time.

Zoe was fifteen when her parents divorced, a stressful event not only because of the separation but because of the secrets she learned about her family at the time; her sister, for instance, was a half-sister who had a different father from herself, and her father had been having an affair for a number of years. At first Zoe lived with her mother and reacted by staying out all night, taking huge risks with her life and generally becoming out of control. After a year it was decided she should live with her dad, a change she welcomed as she and his partner got on well together. Both adults talked to her and together they agreed to certain limits. Zoe was encouraged to take her exams again, and with their help she did well and decided to stay on at school. For her the separation of her parents had very good consequences.

As a group teenagers are vulnerable because they grieve as children, but at the same time are beginning to gain an understanding of the adult world, an awareness of which is linked to concern for themselves as adults, and includes anxiety about whether they can make close relationships in the future and especially whether they will manage to be happy.

'They have cheated me out of my childhood', said a fifteen-year-old girl, expressing a fairly general feeling of teenagers, who are more likely to be directly angry with their parents. 'You don't care about me, you have betrayed me', they say as they fail to take care of themselves, scratching their bodies and making themselves bleed, failing to eat, or abusing themselves in more harmful ways. They feel different from their peers whose parents live together, both older and wiser, but many have a stormy adolescence; they don't belong anywhere. The changeable moods are difficult to deal with, especially by the parent the teenager feels is in the wrong. Teenagers should leave parents, they believe, not the other way round. They may respond by detaching themselves from the situation at home and using their peer group to give them prestige and a sense of belonging; but whereas this is a normal, healthy stage of development providing parents are some-where in the background, in this situation it can contain the seeds of trouble.

Girls may respond in a quieter way than boys. As well as their sadness they can feel rejected by their father and this leads to their hating all men, or Mum for not keeping Dad at home, or themselves. Most children have great concern for one or both parents, are anxious about how they will manage, and often show more concern for their parents than parents do for them at this time. But as well as their grief and anxiety there is a fear that they will be replaced by the children of their parent's partner, or by the partner him- or herself.

But some opt out, desperate to leave the stresses behind and to spend time with their peer group where they belong and are valued. Gilly, aged seventeen, hoping for higher education, reluctantly tried to do this. When her father left her mother for a woman just a few years older than Gilly, her mother's anger knew no bounds and to Gilly and her young sister it seemed as if her mother was going mad in her grief. She constantly screamed and shouted at her daughters, made them go to bed very early, and banned Gilly from seeing friends at weekends, which had been her pattern. Gilly, who described her mother as like one of the three witches in *Macbeth*, could no longer concentrate on her studies and, full of bitterness, feeling she had lost both parents at the same time, left home to live with a much older boyfriend. She talked of her 'forfeited childhood'.

Teenagers can feel embarrassed by the obvious sexuality of their parent with a new partner. Small acts can be upsetting; 'They kissed each other in the street; it was disgusting', said one. Parents can seem more like other teenagers than the parent they want. These teenagers are anxious, too, about their own relationships. Will it be possible for them to have a happy marriage? Might they be betrayed? Who can you trust? They have lost confidence in their ability to be happy and, in common with children of all ages, their self-esteem has plummeted, and this will bring difficulties in concentration which can affect their educational achievements, at least temporarily.

# 4    Children's Reactions: Emotions

Many of the emotions children feel have been referred to already, especially their sadness and anger, which come across so powerfully to anyone helping children come to terms with parental separation. But it is necessary to discuss them more fully as they lie at the heart of this book. The order in which emotions are experienced will vary from child to child and will not be common to all. Nevertheless, it is important to think about the possibilities.

## Conflicting Feelings

Emotions are not clear-cut with a direct relation between cause and effect. For example, a child trying to come to terms with separated parents is involved in an accident which could, to an outsider, be described as 'careless'. In reality his failure to take care of himself may be a result of a feeling of despair or be related to an unconscious hope that his parents would unite in concern. But an event like this could be an attempt, again unconscious, to provoke rows between parents, and in that way to keep their relationship alive. Somewhere mixed up with his feelings there might be an attempt to manipulate the situation between parents – 'It's your fault. You shouldn't have let him ....' 'No, its yours because if you had given him the money to ...'. 'I can't get them together', thinks the child, 'but at least I can get them arguing; it's not what I want but at least I'm not completely powerless.' It is easy to assume there is only one explanation for an event and ignore others, and this has to be remembered when emotions are described separately; the links between the different feelings should not be overlooked.

Certain situations are common to many children but the way they are handled can be crucial for their peace of mind and for the long-term consequences. Take, for example, children who do not want to keep in contact with the non-resident parent; these do not form a large proportion but, to judge from my own experience, many of them are more likely than others to have conflicting feelings; they are hurt and angry but are desperate to see Dad again, to make up, to love and be loved. 'I hate my dad but I want to see him', is a sentiment fairly often expressed by children, though those who have experienced domestic violence may not have such ambivalent feelings.

Samantha, a teenager, was more explicit about her mixed feelings. She was the only one of three sisters who loved her father and visited him. She said he was not a very responsible person and drank too much and was aggressive, but he liked the 'modern' clothes she wore and his pleasure in her looks restored her confidence in herself. She was aware that by seeing him she 'wound Mum up' – something she did because her mum said nasty things about her dad. Nevertheless, it was her mum she respected most because she was aware of the struggle it had been for her to keep the family together and to survive Dad's attempts to undermine her; for instance, by his threats to sell the house. It seemed that in this family of destructive parents Samantha had managed not only to be loyal to her mother and father but had also demonstrated that she was not powerless – she was able to play her part in the situation.

For some the feeling of being rejected by Dad when he left are just too strong to overcome if no explanation has been forthcoming and the child's feelings about the change were not discussed or understood. The child might think: 'Daddy went just when I needed him most. It was me he left, not Mummy.' Young children, especially, quite frequently make this interpretation, and believe it was because either he didn't love them, or they were naughty or rude or just horrible. They are angry with him because the alternative is unbearable sadness, but their distress is secondary to their great need of this very important person in their life. The love they feel for him is a stronger feeling than the anger.

These apparent contradictions are an important part of a child's thinking at this time, although children do not have a monopoly of this kind of confusion – adults too are keenly aware of this amalgam of emotions. Children are less used to using words to express feelings and are likely to lack the vocabulary to do so fully, something which has to be allowed for in trying to understand what they are trying to convey.

Some of the young children can be extremely sad, yearning for Dad as they watch through the window for hours hoping to hear the sound of his car. Their anger may be directed towards Mum because she failed to keep Dad at home, but this can change before long and Dad becomes the bad person. The uncertainty of children's feelings is indicated by a study in Scotland of children between the ages of four and thirteen; half of them could not say which parent they thought was to blame (Mitchell 1985, p. 108). Children talk about a number of reactions and emotions more frequently than others; they tend to be linked inextricably one with the other.


## Disbelief and Denial

The first reaction on the part of many children may be denial because the thing most feared has become reality. The child might think that this couldn't really be happening to him and when he gets home from school Dad will be there. A small child in this phase of disbelief might hide in dark places or display behaviour which he has grown out of in his attempt to find comfort. He knew things were bad, but not so bad as to break up the family. How could he have stopped it? The hope that parents will be united can last many years and survive despite parents being remarried and having new families. This is especially so when changes in the family which affect the child have not been discussed openly, but when there is some acceptance that the separation will be permanent, loss and sadness are likely to dominate.


## Sadness, Loss and Loneliness

The feeling of loss which most children have to deal with can affect a number of different areas of their lives. They have a parent with whom they are not in daily contact, and quite often there is a corresponding reduction in contact with members of their extended family. They could have lost their family home, their school, friends and leisure activities. Less tangible is the loss of their security; it is difficult for them to look ahead and because their image of being an intact family has gone, their self-esteem plummets. They feel different and a target for other children's unkindness. 'At school the big boys bully me, but Miss doesn't take any notice', they say. In many families there is less money to spend on the things children want and for some the joy of living leaves them, until their family begins to recover.

Small children know all too well the feeling of wanting what they cannot have but for them grief is too overwhelming to comprehend. They still believe in magic and find it incomprehensible that a parent could care for them when he or she lives away; for them caring means contact. That limited perception extends to the new relationships separated parents develop, which inevitably result in a number of changes in the family and a very disruptive life for children (Cockett and Tripp 1994). They can become fond of the new partner and his or her family, only to have to face another separation if the relationship should fail. It is this which is thought to cause significant long-term harm to children. Younger ones, of course, are more likely on general grounds to experience more changes in family patterns.

Sadness is the expression of loss and is perhaps the most pervasive emotion felt by children whose parents separate; it can be shown directly by crying or indirectly by actions. The child often experiences waves of grief which envelop her, making it impossible for her to think of anything else, or to concentrate at school. The problem is compounded when the grief is not shared by either parent: one of them might be happy to have found a new partner; the other angry at being badly treated. It is in this sense that separation can be more difficult for a child than bereavement, where the sorrow is experienced and shared by everyone in the family. Children whose sadness is not shared frequently experience a feeling of great loneliness.

Despite times when the child 'seems to have got over it' the despair will leave her feeling hopeless; life is not worth living, there is a shortage of energy and a withdrawal from normal activity. Some fear losing the second parent if they talk too openly about their distress. If that is how the child feels, mourning for the departed parent will be private, painful and unresolved, the child feeling that she alone holds the sadness for the family, in secret.

When, in time, the intensity of the yearning for the non-resident parent declines, grief no longer dominates the child's feelings, confidence returns, favourite activities are enjoyed again and the child begins to grow physically. The process is likely to be speeded up if the sadness can be expressed when it is felt, and the time taken to recover is appreciated by the family. Some families have a taboo on expressing sadness and many, especially fathers, think it is a sign of weakness if boys cry. Feelings are neither good nor bad; they are just feelings which are not helped by an angry response or put-down or by pretending they don't exist.

### Depression

A simplistic view of depression is that it is unexpressed anger but it is far more than that; a depressed person feels isolated and lonely. Children talk about being behind a wall or locked in a room, unable to be reached by anyone. Another characteristic sign is their lack of self-esteem; their unhappy isolation drives away friends. They are fearful, not least through their experience of angry adults; they are not allowed to be outwardly angry themselves, or are frightened to express the feelings they have because they are unacceptable in a child.

Depression, which in varying degrees is a fairly general reaction immediately following separation, sometimes results from a recurring question in a child's head – 'Why has this happened to me?' But given positive influences, notably understanding parents and supportive adults, in due course they will feel better, with girls often recovering more quickly than boys. This process may take a year or more, or perhaps less if the children concerned received an early experience of successful bonding in their first year of life and, in consequence, have a personality capable of recovering.

Children as young as seven or eight can feel suicidal and sometimes act on this feeling, especially if they believe no one cares about them. They may not be rejected, but this is how some of them feel at this time. If they died the absent parent might be sorry and suffer as they have been suffering.

Children who respond by freezing emotionally and becoming unable to progress to the next phase of their development, or regress to a previous one, are often depressed; they have temporarily lost their enjoyment of life, feeling nothing is good. To borrow a metaphor from an understanding psychologist, Dorothy Rowe, they do not see the diamond but the black cushion on which it is placed. Some lose their appetite and can have sleep problems. At home one parent has left them and nobody understands the magnitude of their loneliness; at school they are miserable and no longer fun, with the result that other children ignore them, causing them to feel lonely here too. It will take a mighty effort for them to come out of their trough of despair – something they will be able to do more quickly if they share their distress with somebody.

'It isn't like dying,' explained one small boy whose dad had left him and his mother, 'Dad had a choice, and he didn't choose me.' How can a child find words to say that he feels rejected or not valued or is having to come to terms with broken promises, fallen idols, lost childhood?

We do not know what was in the mind of four-year-old Clive when, after his dad had not kept a promise to come and see him, this cautious little boy rode his tricycle into a main road and was killed instantly. A possibility is that this change from his normal behaviour may have been simply a lapse of concentration because he was wholly preoccupied with his feelings of being rejected. It might have been a desperate sense of sadness and loss or it might have been to do with wanting his dad to suffer as he had; he could have felt that he was not worth anyone caring about him, therefore there was no point in caring about himself and keeping safe. Alternatively it might have been related to depression; without his beloved dad, life for him at this time was really not worth living. We do not know whether the little boy had given other messages about his disturbed state of mind which had not been appreciated. The child's relatives are left saying 'If only ...' and wondering if anything could have been done to prevent such a tragedy.

## Anger

Anger and its causes will have a history. The feelings of insecurity, rejection, failure and of being undermined, which are often allied, do not start when parents separate. The pattern is long-standing, and the type of reaction, whether of hostility or retreat, also pre-dates the divorce. Children may have felt angry with their parents for a long time because when they were small their needs were not met. Without love and care they could have failed to make a satisfactory attachment; subsequently they could have been rejected or treated harshly. Some will have experienced fear through the expression of hostility between their parents. If these are familiar situations to them, then the separation can be the catalyst for their anger.

The feeling of powerlessness and having no control over important family issues is related and often linked to anger, or it can be a cover-up for despair and sadness which threatens to be too crushing if expressed at all. It is easier to be angry than sad and people are more likely to respond to it. For children it may mask a sense of not being valued; a child might think: 'If they cared for me they wouldn't have separated' or 'If they really loved me they wouldn't ignore my wishes; nobody listens.' Their experience has taught them, rightly or wrongly, that to your parents you don't matter, and it's not fair because everyone else has an ordinary family.

Someone feeling attacked, unloved, undermined or inadequate, might displace the feeling on to someone else and make him or her angry. You, the child, are really angry with the parent who has left you but it is not safe to express this because if you did then he (or sometimes she) might never want to see you again and although visits are not always enjoyable, he is your dad and in a sense belongs to you. Dad's girlfriend then could be the target for your anger; she is slightly less risky to attack than Dad and by doing so you are attempting to hide your own unacceptable feelings of jealousy, as she has become a rival and stolen your dad. Alternatively the feeling can be displaced on to Mum who, in your eyes, should have behaved differently or done something to keep Dad at home. At other times children blame both parents, who, as they see it, selfishly didn't think of the children at all but just did what they wanted to do.

Paul, aged nine, behaved like a much younger child. After the separation he demonstrated quite manic behaviour, was very amused by his own unfunny remarks and obsessed with anything to do with defecation. Lacking social skills he did not have any friends, but was often in trouble which he said invariably had been caused by other boys. 'They pushed me and I fell against someone else. It wasn't my fault.' He responded with anger to being teased but at the same time invited it to happen, his behaviour making him an easy target; the numerous incidents at school served to get him attention, though not the sort he really wanted. He said he felt OK about his family but he hated his dad – no he didn't, he loved him; he hated his dad's girlfriend. He had vivid memories of Dad hitting him and of parental rows over many years and although very angry with his father he could not express it directly. The anger was in part on his mother's behalf because his father had left home to live with his mother's best friend, but he also had a powerful reason of his own: he hated his dad making disparaging remarks about his mother which he did not believe he could stop. Paul was an angry, unhappy boy without the skill to evoke sympathy in others.

Paul's story reveals one way in which children express their feelings outside the family; others do so in more antisocial ways by resorting to bullying other children or taking their property. Dave had organized quite a sophisticated system of blackmail, demanding money from smaller boys in return for not beating them up. With the support of the school counsellor and his parents he was helped to find a better solution to his problem, which was one of low-esteem; he was an example of a child, not normally in trouble, who was attempting to deal with feelings of powerlessness and loss in an unacceptable way. His thinking might have been that by making waves, his parents would know that he hadn't sunk without trace, and it was better to be angry than depressed. As one child said, 'It is a way of avoiding an awful feeling of numbness, almost like being a nobody.' There are, of course, quite other reasons for this type of behaviour, some of them unconscious and quite complicated, but for these children it was designed to bring Dad back home again or to deal with Dad's leaving.

A child may become angry because of his awareness that he is being used in the emotional battles between his parents, and particularly if he has some inkling that one parent has a hidden agenda to destroy his relationship with the other; the unspoken threat, one that creates great fear, is that if you take your dad's side you will endanger your relationship with your mum.

Children who are unable to express anger openly because of their personality or the family's belief that it is unacceptable, might experience personal failure: 'I can't do anything right'; 'Nobody likes me'; 'Nobody gives me anything'; 'Everyone has got one, except me.'

Feelings like these serve to avoid the dangerous activity of blaming parents who are powerful and can retaliate by rejection and mask the belief that if a parent doesn't want you then nobody else will. Here depression and anger intertwine. Both of them can cause sleeplessness. Fear and angry images of revenge can grow in the silence of the night. They suffer terrible nightmares related to being absolutely alone and abandoned, or angry crocodiles are trying to bite them and no one is near to help. For a time, bizarre and scary thoughts can be a nightly torture for these troubled children. Victim and attacker merge. These are what children describe so vividly.

It can be useful, in thinking about anger, to divide its expression into one of three energy zones (Jewett 1997). Children whose primary zone is their mouth will suck their hand, chew paper, bite their nails or objects such as pencils or clothes. They will also shout and use verbal abuse. Those whose primary zone is their hands will break things, tear paper or clothes, pull out their hair, threaten with fists, punch and hit. Those who use their feet will run, kick and stamp. The point of these groupings is to suggest approved outlets which involve the energy zone used. It may be possible to help, for example, the child who hits by encouraging him to hit his hand with his fist while shouting 'I'm getting really angry.' Another safe way of dealing with angry feelings was described by a child who went intó her bedroom and threw toys and papers everywhere then, when she was exhausted, went downstairs and ate chocolates. Nobody was harmed and it helped her feel better, at least temporarily.

For some, anger can be delayed, only being brought into the open when it is safe to do so, or when a child feels she no longer has to protect her parents. It is an emotion which is more easily expressed in relation to trivial things but in reality is frequently about very important feelings which can't be talked about with the people who are most involved, because of their different perspective and because to talk about true feelings could easily make things worse.

Children may be less dominated by anger if they are aware of what is causing the feeling, and are encouraged to express it in a way which does not harm others. They may then break the pattern because they are learning to have some control and are receiving attention for acceptable behaviour. Nevertheless, there is always the possible risk – not necessarily common – of their repeating the example of failed adult relationships because they have not had first-hand experience of living in a loving family and have never learnt how to deal with differences in a positive way. The good experience needed to change the pattern of angry response is sometimes the remarriage of the resident parent, provided the event is a happy experience for the child.

There is a positive side to anger; it can act as a stimulus to make changes in thinking and doing. It can lead to better ways of reacting which do not hurt anyone or cause damage, including to oneself. It might help a child find a way of putting the anger outside herself if she can share it with someone she trusts. Or she may be able to use it as a spur to fight back by not letting her parents get her down – she will show them they can't hurt her anymore, she is not going to let it undermine her, and she will do well at school. These attitudes can direct anger into fighting low self-esteem, utilizing it to a productive end and thereby gaining a new confidence. Given perseverance and courage, it gives the power to make changes, to do well and in the end to be happy.

## Guilt

Guilt is like several other emotions in being closely related to the complex feeling which is anger. Thus some children, full of guilt and the self-hate that often accompanies it, are difficult to control because they want to be punished; this is what they feel they deserve because of their bad thoughts. And they believe either that they caused the split or that they could have helped stop it happening. It is perhaps the most difficult emotion for parents to deal with because at least one parent is likely to be angry or guilty too, for different reasons. Their own pain and the difficulties of their new situation can make them unable to notice the distress of the child.

Guilt can also result from the tendency of some children to blame themselves for the separation. As eight-year-old Andrew explained, 'Dad said he would leave us if we didn't stop arguing about the television. We argued the next day and now he has gone. The worst bit of it is that neither of us wanted to see the programme but we have to argue about everything. It's how we are; it doesn't mean anything to us, but now look what we've done. I feel so bad about it. My brother says Dad would have left anyway, but I don't think so. When I asked Dad about it he told me not to be so silly, so I haven't asked about it again.'

Guilty feelings can be imposed by unthinking parents. Nat was an eight-year-old enjoying a very close relationship with his dad, who had been working abroad doing a dangerous job. On his return he did not go back to the marital home, saying that they were too noisy and he needed peace and quiet. Nat and his sister were told a number of lies before they realized that their dad had left for good and in fact had been having an affair for some time. Nat was devastated. He had been very worried about his dad getting killed and longing for him to come home;

to be told at first that he was to blame for this not happening, then finding out that this was a lie – and his dad's lie, at that – although he could not accept that it wasn't his fault, and then finally having to accept that his dad had left him for good, made him very sad indeed.

Nat and his mother were united by tears and sadness. This desperately lonely small boy made a fairly serious attempt on his life, perhaps because for him life didn't seem worth living without Dad. This didn't succeed but it did alert his mother to the depth of his despair and she found someone he could talk to in confidence. By this time his grief had turned to anger which had not diminished his love for his dad. 'I hate him, he told me lies and didn't love me so he left me – but I want to see him more often and I want him to love me.' Too often parents believe that if they reject their children, that child will reject them, and too often this is not so; many children of divorce grow up retaining a longing for their dad to give them some sign that they are special to him, and are constantly disappointed.

### Anxiety, Fear and Confusion

Anxiety and confusion are usually related to future situations, though past events are not forgotten and play a part. In this respect they differ from anger which is likely to be caused by past, and sometimes present, events.

Experience teaches many children that adults cannot be trusted and do not consider their wishes and feelings; instead, events happen and they are left to try to make sense of the mixed messages they receive. In the attempt to reduce this confusion they pick up information from overhearing telephone conversations, reading other people's letters and listening to adults talking – and may find cousins quite a good source of information as they are able to pass on interesting details overheard from the less inhibited discussions in their own home.

#### Anxiety About Each Parent
Children talk about certain anxieties more often than others. First and foremost is concern about their parents. How will Dad manage alone? Will he feed himself? Will he be lonely? How will Mum manage? Will she be able to mend things and do the garden? If she is sad, will she be able to cope with herself, the house, and the children? Will she get ill or have an accident? Or, even more worrying, will it all be too much for her and will she leave or commit suicide? Many children have a fear of being abandoned in the night, of waking up in an empty house, completely alone. Others share their mother's anxiety about being poor.

*Anxiety About the Parents' Relationship*
Many children are weighed down with different adult worries: Dad hasn't paid money for the children's maintenance and Mum says he could go to prison; they are arguing about who should have the stereo and whether the children can go to Disneyland. Another great fear is that Mum or Dad might each get married again and will begin a new life maybe with children from the new partner or maybe they will have their own baby, then who will want me? Anybody? 'Dad wants me to love his new girlfriend's child but I hate her because Dad makes such a fuss of her. I hate the girlfriend too because she won't let Dad see me without her. Sometimes I am so lonely.' One child expressed his feeling of not being wanted by saying that he thought he had reached his sell-by date.

*Anxiety About Themselves*
Where children are involved in hostile separations their fears relate to intensely personal danger. They may be afraid of being abducted from school, a fear which can be based on reality. Even more worrying for a little girl, Amy, was the time when she was told by her dad that he would come in the night and kill her mummy with a knife if he was stopped from seeing Amy. Nowhere was safe for her. To induce fear about the warm protective place which is the centre of a child's world is a form of emotional abuse. Often these fears are expressed not only directly but also symbolically, by being afraid of burglars, witches or things being out of control, such as buildings falling down. Obviously, all children have similar fears but it is their intensity which is notable in those whose present home life is insecure.

Parental violence is an all too common experience for children and does not always end with separation; nor is it always physical. Brenda was one such child who lived in fear; her father made it clear that if the court thought he was irresponsible, then that was how he would behave, it would be a good way of getting back at his ex-wife. He told the children that they need not wear seatbelts as he drove recklessly, ignoring the obvious fact that they were frightened and telling them how exciting it was. At other times he took them into pubs and failed to notice when they wandered off, and at each contact visit he told them Mummy was a bad person and one day they would live with him.

Children are generally too frightened to talk about the violence they witness or experience or the abuse they suffer at the hands of their parents. These children can walk a tightrope of divided loyalty and live in constant fear that they will upset one or other parent if they ask about the things which trouble them.

*Anxiety About Their Future*

Children frequently mention their fear of being forgotten or rejected. Perhaps Dad will live too far away to visit and will soon forget them, or Mum will become ill, or perhaps she will leave too. Anxiety extends to how they will manage when they grow up and this can start when they are quite young. If they know other members of their family who have divorced they may come to believe that this is a family pattern which, in due course, will be their fate too. Some resign themselves to this – 'We all get divorced in our family' – others decide that they will never get married. A number of boys express a concern that they may be violent when they grow up because they have lived in a family accustomed to violence.

Anxieties about future changes will almost always be present. 'We might have to leave our house then I shall have to go to a different school and lose my friends. Won't anyone tell me honestly what is going to happen, and why don't they ask me what I think?' Such anxieties can cause deep unhappiness which some children hide behind a smokescreen of trivia. Their drawing of the happy smiling family should not fool anybody.

## Envy

Envy of intact families can be difficult for a child to control. Boys have a vision of every Dad taking his son to watch Manchester United each Saturday; girls might see other people's mums as big sisters who don't insist on bedtime, tidying bedrooms or doing homework. Intact families have lovely holidays and go abroad, have money for a big car and bicycles and nice clothes. Eight-year-old Chris, whose dad left home when he was a baby, had these feelings, understandably, as he had no memory of his dad and had never been taken to the seaside or zoo. There is a risk that those who, for whatever reason, are not treated in the same way as their peers will feel different, inferior and unlovable.

## Relief

Children can feel greatly relieved when they accept that it is all right to have 'bad' feelings because they are human and have had an upsetting experience. Such feelings are just as valid as others, good or bad. They should not be denied or ignored, but expressed in harmless ways; they are a way of dealing with loss and form a part of mourning.

Fortunately, for most children these reactions become less pervasive and, given time, no longer dominate their thinking and allow other feelings to take over. A considerable number of children have told me that although they were very distressed when the separation took place, with the passage of time and the ending of uncertainty, they saw separation as having been the best solution. 'I thought it terrible when Dad left', said ten-year-old Martha, 'but now that Mum and Dad have both made changes in their lives, and are nicer people, I think it was the best thing they could have done for themselves and for us.' This is how many children so placed see things. For them to reach this conclusion requires their acceptance, albeit painful, that the separation is permanent. It is easier for children whose parents retain a relationship of caring and concern despite knowing that they can't live together in harmony.

## Hope

For the children the worst possibility, Mum and Dad splitting up, happened, but even though recovery might have taken two years, everyone has survived. It is often believed that to see both parents is enough, but children need more than this. For them it is the quality of parenting by each one which is crucial; only if they feel they are important to both parents and are loved and supported by them does the future look promising. The other important factor is that they are no longer exposed to parental hostility and fear is removed. If these essentials are in place children will survive well, be happier and will be able to face the future with confidence and hope.

# 5    Domestic Violence: A Family Secret

## Some General Comments

Domestic violence cannot be equated with divorce or separation. Obviously they can be seen as separate issues but in thinking about domestic violence and divorce, the links are too close to discuss one without the other.

Here, domestic violence refers to acts of violence by men on women in their home. Most (but not all) of the perpetrators are fathers or stepfathers; their partners are the victims and although physical abuse is what is usually referred to by the phrase, it encompasses sexual and emotional abuse too. The indications are that a woman is most at risk at two critical times when the relation between the partners is changing; that is, when she is pregnant or when she leaves or has just left the relationship. Children can also be hurt, whether as victims or as observers, or if they are used as weapons by one or other party. Understandably, domestic violence is one of the many matters that families wish to keep secret from the outside world, a secret made easier to keep because of a reluctance by the public generally to acknowledge the extent of violence. However, there are some signs of change and the police are more inclined to take action than they were in the past.

Nevertheless, the extent of domestic violence is still subject to debate. Those who work in refuges, victim support and other similar organizations have no hesitation in saying it is widespread and many believe it is very much under-reported (Saunders 1995). The opponents of this view believe events are exaggerated; that when a woman says she has been the victim of violence there is often no proof, and the accusations could therefore be part of the weaponry she uses to fight the matrimonial war.

One obstacle to confronting the problem of domestic violence, perhaps the principal one, can be easily understood. To intervene in the most private relations of an individual's life, those between couples, and those between parents and their children, is generally seen as an unwarranted intrusion because it impinges on personal morals and ethics. Although there is a growing awareness and understanding of the unhappiness of these families and that the safety of child should be paramount, there is still a long way to go.

## Men

A generation ago a higher proportion of men than at present did dangerous physical work – down the mines, at sea, or in the armed forces, for example – where they relied on each other for their survival. Their self-respect came from being tough and certainly not from any involvement in family life which was thought of as women's work. Although there have been changes in the type of work the majority of men do, some of the old attitudes survive to perpetuate the belief that a man is the head of the family and therefore, in the natural course of events, dominates it; wives might be valued, but they are possessions. These attitudes are being changed and perhaps in the majority of families are no longer the pattern, but to make further headway will involve tackling the root causes of male violence and power, a mammoth task involving education – especially of boys. In parallel with this there would need to be a serious attack on the social causes of family stress arising from poverty which, for disadvantaged families, can aggravate stress.

This does not mean that children of affluent families are not also subjected to domestic violence. Disadvantaged families do not have a monopoly of either men or women with personality defects, serious mental health problems and drink or drug addictions. Aggressive personalities who dominate women and children, perceived as weaker, come from every social class. Hugh was such a father who had been brought up in comparative luxury by a series of nannies. Being sent to boarding school at an early age was an unhappy experience for him as he was bullied by teachers and pupils verbally and physically. He had only known discipline through fear and this is how he related to his own sons, maintaining 'It never did me any harm.' Fortunately, when the two boys decided to run away after a particularly unpleasant incident the authorities were involved and, with family therapy the father came to realize that his way of handling his sons was not acceptable in present-day thinking and he had to make changes. The situation for the boys then became more tolerable.

The problem of domestic violence is not an easy one; men who are violent in all probability have not had a loving role model to emulate when they were growing up although they themselves were not necessarily abused victims of violence as children. It could be that fantasy affected their behaviour and perhaps some of them modelled themselves on television heroes, who depend on strength and violence for success, but they had no direct experience of men who are strong but also gentle and caring to balance these images.

They are at risk of growing up emotionally deprived and angry, maybe with contempt for women, but, as with all emotional handicaps, the situation can improve if there is the will to change and provided they are fortunate enough to receive some positive experiences to fill this early void. But this is mainly conjecture; very little is known about the thoughts and feelings of such men. For aggressive males who can see the need to change, some small-scale projects have been set up which challenge the men's behaviour and examine their attitudes to women.

The break-up of the relationship, especially by the man's partner, is a time when violent men must face failure, and violence can be seen as a response to powerlessness. Men who rule their families by fear or violence usually have little self-esteem and, as a broad generalization, are unable to deal with expressions of anger from others. They have found that violence works and are adept at blaming their victims, maintaining 'She asked for it', or 'Children must be obedient.' Even if he had left her for another woman it does not stop him being very angry with her. If she had been different none of the trouble would have happened, therefore she deserves to be punished. He feels justified in making life as difficult as he can for her in an attempt to hide his vulnerability.

If his wife has walked out on account of his behaviour it can be even more difficult for him. How could his ex-wife do this to him and put him into a situation over which he has no control? The problem for such men is that they cannot deal with being abandoned; some use flattery and fine words to entice their wives to return to them – 'He brought me some flowers, so what could I do?' Others increase their hostility in more subtle ways and may use the children as their allies.

In some families the violence develops in intensity, starting as unpleasant teasing or negative comments which might be an attempt to make the abuser feel better about himself. The situation can then become more aggressive, with the wife being blamed for everything which goes wrong, and told she deserves to be punished. This can be done in a number of ways: by economic abuse – depriving her of money and making her account for every penny she spends; by increasing her isolation – 'You are not on any account to leave the house'; by threats – 'If you phone your sister I'll ...'; by unwanted touching and sexual abuse (rape in marriage is an offence); or by attacking her property. In relationships where violence is more physical than verbal the smack becomes a punch, and when it develops into hitting with an object it can become life-threatening.

## Violence by Others

Fathers and father-figures, although responsible for much of the domestic violence, are not exclusively to blame. Other relatives or baby sitters can be responsible; in some families older brothers are physically violent to their younger siblings, perhaps also sexually abusing them – a situation that, although not common, does happen more often than is appreciated. A number of small-scale studies indicate that if incest is practised there is a strong likelihood of domestic violence occurring (Morley and Mullender 1994, p. 32).

## Women

Numerically, women who are violent to men appear to present a problem but the incidents are usually less severe than male violence against women and less likely to be life-threatening. In some relationships both partners are physically violent to each other, perhaps doing more harm to their children than to themselves by giving them a very strong message that inflicting pain resolves differences. A few women are volatile or violent and unable to meet the need of their children to be kept safe. Others have not had any experience themselves of being cared for by a loving mother, and some are inadequate or aggressive personalities, are mentally ill, or become violent under the influence of alcohol or drugs. Whatever the situation, children cannot fail to be upset and fearful of the outcome.

Many women victims are very grateful for the help given by refuges but those not so fortunate may prefer to become homeless rather than go on living with a violent partner. As a result many women have both physical and mental health problems and the children have severe emotional or behavioural difficulties and developmental delays. They also lack good health care. It is a major problem that affects many children adversely and a permanent solution should be found rather than bed and breakfast hostels or unsuitable rented accommodation. These are short-term expedients which do long-term harm.

Some work in America (Kaufman and Zigler 1987) suggests that there could be a genetic component which leads perpetrators of violence not to be concerned about their victims, and this is a situation compounded by birth difficulties, a lack of bonding and poor post-natal care. It is argued that attention to difficulties before and soon after birth could decrease the amount of later violence dramatically. This genetic approach could possibly be extended to discover, first, why some violent men come from non-violent backgrounds and why a majority of boys from violent homes do not grow up to abuse family members, whereas others do and emulate the behaviour.

Second, it might give an understanding of why a proportion of women, less than half in most studies, have experienced an abusive childhood but do not regard it as a normal pattern of family life and therefore do not repeat the pattern as adults by marrying abusive men (Stark and Flitcraft 1985). However sophisticated future research may be, it would be wrong to seek a single explanation for such a complex relationship as that in which domestic violence is involved.

### Why Didn't You Tell?

An eleven-year-old boy described how his violent father had half-strangled him, leaving bruises on his neck which lasted for days. He had just stopped him from punching his mother, therefore his father had turned on him. The fear in the family was that if they pressed charges the father would be released on bail and on his return home would be even more violent because the police had been told. This is one reason for the reluctance of many victims to involve the authorities until the incidents have become too numerous or too vicious, and even then the chances of the charges being dropped because of insufficient evidence are still high. If this is not the outcome the aggressor is more likely to be charged with common assault rather than more serious charges. Before the authorities take action there have to be indications that significant harm has taken place, something which can be quite difficult to establish. Nevertheless, there is growing awareness of the extent of domestic violence and more women are being courageous enough to inform the police, and there are helping organizations available.

In addition to the fear of further physical abuse, there are other reasons why women may be reluctant to inform the authorities. Violence may not always stop the victim loving the perpetrator and there is always the hope that things will get better. Then there is the belief in the sanctity of marriage which keeps some wives with their violent husbands, a belief which is held strongly by more women than might be thought. For others, the children's need for two parents overrides all other considerations. An additional powerful reason for not telling is when the fear of violence is outweighed by a stronger fear, that in the event of separation the children may want to live with the stronger partner – who is not likely to be the victim.

When women are victims there are usually many incidents of violence before they decide there can be no more forgiving and starting again. These victims have remained in the abusive relationship for a variety of reasons, the dominant one being fear of more violence, but the greater worry might be managing on their own without help or money, while many are simply very apprehensive of unknown consequences, especially if children are involved.

Some mothers are ever hopeful that this will be the last time they will be hurt or that their partner will miraculously change. Another widespread belief among mothers is that if the authorities knew about the violence they themselves would be blamed for not protecting the children, who would then be taken away. A woman can also be afraid that if she were to reveal the full extent of the violence it might result in her partner being imprisoned, a result difficult to contemplate if the children love their dad regardless of what he does. They might blame her for putting him in prison; and one day he would be released – then what?

Women who as children were both loved and beaten may have learnt that it is all right to hit the people you love, therefore their violent partner really loves them. There are a small proportion who, it can be surmised, have a psychological problem which predisposes them to see the violence as favourable, whether as evidence of attention or perhaps what they deserve; for them, it is better than being ignored.

Some mothers have lost any trust they might have had with those empowered to help and, fearful of the consequences if the extent of the aggression becomes known outside the family, deny that it happened. 'It's all right. It's not serious and he says he won't do it again.' A child who witnessed his mother being thrown down the stairs by his father hears his mother telling her neighbour she fell downstairs. What does he think? More secrets; more lies; how do you make sense of it all? How do you put it out of your mind?

**Protecting Women**

The indications from a number of sources suggest that the most helpful intervention for women and children who are experiencing violence is to accept that a mother should be with her children, supported and safe, possibly in a refuge or adequate housing, unless the abuser is removed from the home under an emergency protection order. In other words, to protect women is frequently the most effective way to protect children (Kelly 1994, p. 53). But besides practical help emotional support is required; the mother needs to believe that the professional people involved are on her side because to make such a major change as leaving a frightening, abusive man takes great courage.

## A 'Cycle of Violence'?

A number of reasons have been advanced to explain aggressive behaviour in a domestic setting, of which the 'cycle of violence' is the most popular. It is alleged that those who grow up in violent families become violent adults or victims of violence, and may abuse their children. Most of the studies are retrospective; that is, abusers and victims are asked about their childhood and the lapse of years may make the memories unreliable. There is no evidence to suggest this belief has a firm base (Rutter and Madge 1976; Morley and Mullender 1994). It is a view which contains an element of resignation, and the opinion that not a lot can be done. In fact what can be done involves looking at the social assumptions about the power structure between men and women, something which requires a fundamental shift in thinking.

## Smacking Children

Violence against children is a continuum; it can start with a tap on the hand to stop a child touching something forbidden, develop into hitting with the hand, go on to involve the use of an object and finally result in a vicious onslaught, which at that stage is called domestic violence.

Hitting children may be a part of their parents' relationship with them, a part they see as normal. As children say: 'This is what dads and mums do.' Quite often they differentiate between smacking and punching; they expect to be smacked for wrongdoing but punching is unacceptable and hitting with an object such as a stick or belt is seen as severe punishment. The consensus of opinion amongst adults in Britain (including the government) is still that hitting a child, providing it is not too hard, is acceptable. For some adults, inflicting physical pain, however moderate, could be a part of child-rearing that is difficult to relinquish because to do so would mean opposing the belief and practice of their own parents.

This is a firmly held conviction despite the awareness that there are other ways of parenting based on respect and co-operation and children's desire to please. But children also have to be taught limits and to learn that some things are too dangerous, or that for whatever reason they cannot have what they want. Tone of voice indicating disapproval may be enough and it may be necessary to follow this up with action, but inflicting any physical pain would be alien in this approach. Positive parenting is similar but has to include giving the child clear messages about unacceptable behaviour. In order seriously to decrease the amount of domestic violence it is necessary to tackle the vexed question of hitting children to control them, otherwise the problem continues, affecting the next generation.

As has been said before, the relationship between man and wife or parent and child is personal, and no government which passes laws forbidding smacking can enforce it in every case, but this is no reason for not passing such legislation. What it does is to give a lead by conveying the message that this practice is not acceptable and those who continue to use violence on children are disapproved of by society generally. This was the result in Sweden where Swedish law provided an impetus to changing public opinion. In my opinion such action would make a major contribution to reducing the amount of domestic violence in Britain.

# 6 Domestic Violence: The Children

The Children Act 1989 stated that local authorities have a duty to prevent children suffering abuse and that they should not be subjected to 'significant harm'. These were important steps forward, but ten years on children are still being violently treated although there is some awareness of other more hidden manifestations of abuse which are not covered by the Act and which are far more difficult to prove. Police, magistrates, some doctors and mediators are often unwilling to acknowledge the extent of the occurrence of all kinds of abuse and their effects on children. A number of factors contribute to this reluctance, not least that many people have difficulty in believing that a child's pain could be inflicted by fathers or father-figures and that, where there is domestic violence, it will cause both emotional and physical hurt.

At the time of writing, it was reported that a five-year-old girl was beaten to death and the mother's partner found guilty. Neither the police nor social services acted on the information known to them that domestic violence was taking place; nobody talked to the child alone. Although this incident does not relate specifically to children of divorce it serves to illustrate the reluctance of the adults involved to take children's comments seriously or to talk to child victims directly.

It is estimated that in Britain about seven out of ten men who beat their wives also physically abuse their children; research from America, Australia and Denmark supports this assertion (Saunders 1995). Without doubt the problem is widespread and serious; in three months in 1997 Lancashire Family Mediation Service found that more than a quarter of those referred to them had criminal records pertaining to offences of violence or offences against children; the implications for staff safety were taken seriously (Gray 1998). At the extremity of domestic violence, many more children are killed by family members than the six or so a year who die at the hands of strangers, though normally less publicity is given to these tragedies.

The extent is difficult to contemplate. In recent years the Department of Health has received 120 notifications annually of child deaths or incidents of serious harm to children usually resulting from physical assault and/or neglect by one or both parents or step-parents.

A large proportion of those responsible are fathers or stepfathers who have a history of violence towards their female partners as well as towards the child (James 1994).

What distinguishes domestic violence to children is the power of one party, the parent, and the powerlessness of the other, the child. The same applies to other weaker members of the family, but there is a particular ethical issue when children are involved. A child learns as much by the force of example as by instruction, and the message that violence is a proper means of controlling social behaviour is generally regarded as undesirable.

At present, though, because domestic violence is seen to be largely a private matter, and because it is so horrific for many of us, we want to distance ourselves from it, to pretend it doesn't happen and to believe the adult's story that it was just an accident, rather than to believe what children say. If we do not see and accept it, we won't feel so bad about not checking the facts or not taking action. Children also contribute to the silence, usually through fear of the abuser, but also because they think that the consequences of disclosure are unknown and could easily be worse than their present experience. A third reason might be that they think they are to blame.

### The Extent of the Problem

When discussing domestic violence it has to be remembered that in many separations there is no violence or control by power. The marriage has failed for quite other reasons, and in some families violence only began after the separation. According to Cockett and Tripp (1994), this is especially stressful for the children as they can be more directly involved, either because the hostility concerns them through issues such as contact, or because they are enrolled as messengers between parents. The authors suggest that the number of changes that children experience in the family is likely to have a more serious effect than conflict, and in their opinion the loss of a parent by separation is not likely to be the most important adverse factor. The conflicting views suggest that whichever of these factors is present there is more likelihood of later difficulties. However, where there is violence, and women and children are living in fear, it needs to be given priority. Many incidents are seen or heard by children, a situation which can pre-date separation, often for a number of years.

In Exeter a quarter of children of divorce had experienced domestic violence in their family but the authors of the research suggest that violence, although associated with low self-image, is not as damaging as the loss of a parent by separation (Cockett and Tripp 1994). This view is not accepted by all writers; for example, Rodgers and Pryor (1998) concluded that conflict contributes to a negative outcome, as do multiple changes of family composition.

Reviews of research suggest that 40–60 per cent of children are physically abused in homes where domestic violence is perpetrated against the women partners (Morley and Mullender 1994); even those children who are not physically hurt cannot fail to be affected emotionally by their experience. Some are aware of the non-physical forms of abuse and controlling behaviour that have been used. A dominant man may encourage or force a child to participate in physical assaults on his mother or in verbal denigration of her. In other families threats to harm children are used to control mothers; or a man, besides being violent to his wife, might beat his child in order to dominate her. Children can be used in other ways: one father strangled his child's much-loved gerbil, saying, 'You can tell your mother that if she tries to stop me seeing you, next time it will be her.'

## The Link With Sexual Abuse

Where a child is physically abused at home it is likely that the mother is being treated in the same way. There are also indications that the man who controls his family by violence or by fear, which can be by small non-verbal threatening signals, may also be sexually abusing family members including children, but this is often not disclosed until the woman and her children feel safe in a refuge.

One sample of 116 children who were suspected targets of sexual abuse reported that 45 per cent of the mothers in their study had been abused by their male partner (Stark and Flitcraft 1985). ChildLine confirmed the view that if mothers were abused, children could be too and if there was domestic violence in the family, sexual abuse of children should not be ruled out. ChildLine also found that many children described both sexual and physical assaults beginning after parents had separated (MacLeod 1996) and they warn that the possibility of a child being sexually abused should never be ignored in households which contain a violent man (ChildLine 1998, p. 27).

They also found that research studies on child abuse have consistently noted the connection between domestic violence and child abuse and that there is a higher correlation between these two family patterns than almost any other single factor.

### Reactions and Feelings of Children

*Anxiety*

Worry about Mum, and sometimes about Dad, takes a great deal of the emotional energy of children. This applies not only to physical violence but also to other behaviour designed to dominate through fear, such as restraint, deprivation of money or food, social isolation and other forms of emotional abuse. Because they have witnessed or been included in such displays of power, and they feel so powerless themselves, they have had, or taken, too much responsibility and grow up too quickly.

Often, these troubled children lack basic security and joy in their life and feel cheated. Many are constantly watchful – 'frozen watchfulness' is a good phrase to describe this – ready to act if the violence becomes life-threatening. One seven-year-old said 'I haven't got a place to hide.' These are children who have to suppress their own feelings because of fear, and survive by becoming tense, forever trying to be as invisible as possible. They learn to gauge the father's mood by the way he enters the house and they are aware of the signs that Mum is having a bad day. Cathy becomes Catherine, Andy is called Andrew, the tone of the mother's voice is slightly higher and they know this is the day they will do nothing right, however much they try to avoid trouble.

They also know that the trigger for violence can be very small. Sara was adept at knowing what mood her dad was in when he returned from the pub. 'It was one Sunday after dinner and Dad had just come back. He told me to wash up and without thinking I said "Just a minute, I've very nearly finished my homework." Dad went mad and blamed mum for not controlling us children. I'd rather he had thrown me across the room, not her.'

Others talk of never feeling safe, of never being free from anxiety, and even at school concentration is difficult because of worries about what is happening at home. As in a number of the domestic situations described in this book, confidence is likely to be affected and there can be difficulty in making friends because of low self-esteem. The other strong feeling children have is to blame themselves for Dad's violence.

*Revenge*

One boy having difficulties at school said he couldn't wait until he was bigger so that he could beat up his dad. This is a boy who lives with a constant fear that one day his dad will kidnap him from school, but his long-term anxiety, shared by a number of boys, is that he will grow up to be violent because he has known so much violence already.

*Conflicting Feelings*
It is difficult to separate the effects of the divorce itself from that of violence in marriage, as many of the children's reactions to distress are similar, but what is indisputable is the conflicting feelings that result, most of which are not expressed because they do not feel it is safe to do so. 'I love Dad but I hate him because of the way he treats Mum.' 'I love Dad but I'm afraid of him.' 'I hate Dad but I wish he would come back home.' Love and violence are intertwined with the risk that this could be the pattern a child takes into adulthood.

Alex, aged seven, was such a child. Even four years after the event he has a recurring vision of his father in the kitchen, wielding a wooden rolling pin and smashing it down on his mother's head. She was taken to hospital in an ambulance and Alex did not see her for some days. His work at school suffered and despite his obsessive flashbacks of the horror of the scene he still wanted to see his father. He said it would not happen again because his dad loved him and if it did happen he would be put in prison for a long time and his dad would never be allowed to see him again. Alex admitted he was a bit frightened of his dad but not enough to forgo the contact – and the treats – his dad provided.

Confusion is also present in children's minds: 'Why is it like this?' They answer their own question with such explanations as illness, worry about money, loss of a job, a special family member or even pets. These situational explanations hide deeper, painful questions: 'Can Dad really love me if he hurts me?' 'If Mum really loved us why doesn't she leave him?' But the general feeling children have is that this is the situation they know and have learned to live with. At times, in their eyes, splitting up the family is not a good solution; at other times they wish very much that this would happen.

*Factors Affecting Children's Reactions*
There is much to be learned about children's reactions to domestic violence in their family and more needs to be known about violent mothers as well as fathers. How severely the children are affected must be influenced by their age and personality and especially by their resilience and ability to leave the stress behind when they are at school or involved in other activities. But also relevant is their own relationship with the abuser. If fear dominates, the degree of violence they have witnessed and whether they have suffered violence themselves have probably less effect than the fact that it is happening at all. The previous and ongoing relationship with both parents and the methods used to inflict discipline and control can be significant as

well. In some families the mother is a victim as well as the children, whereas in others mothers support the father in his harshness. There can be little doubt that the second instance would be comparatively more harmful for the children.


## The Importance of Talking

Sally, hearing her mother screaming, ran downstairs to find her cowering in a corner of the living room, her face wracked with pain and her father standing over her. Her pregnant mother was subsequently taken to hospital by ambulance. When Sally talked about the incident a year after it happened she explained what a dilemma she was in: her mum said her dad had deliberately kicked her in the stomach a number of times but her dad said he had slipped and he hadn't meant to hurt her mother. Sally did not know who to believe. One of her parents was lying. Which one? On the one hand, she was reluctant to believe that her father could be so violent; but, on the other, she did not want to believe that her mother told her lies. She did not want to have to make a judgement but gained some relief through talking about her dilemma. By doing so the incident became a little more distant from her and thinking about it became less obsessive.

Children who talk about domestic violence do so with tremendous heartache and merely thinking about various incidents can make them cry even though they happened many years before. The relief some of the children gain just by sharing these experiences is justification enough for giving them the opportunity to do so. It is simply not true that they are making up the incidents and it is simply not true that if they are ignored the children 'will get over it'. Words and drawings can be used to modify the experience in a way which can lead to it being faced; not forgotten, but absorbed. The torment and obsessive thoughts relating to the event decrease and, provided the child has some explanation which will help her understand something about it and which is honest, in time the event can be contained without pain.


## Coping Strategies

A different way of dealing with anxiety is to leave it to a sibling (usually older) to handle while they get on with their own lives. David, a teenager, did this; he believed that when his parents finally split up for good, after a number of temporary separations, he would be better off with his father despite knowing he was a violent man. He did not defend his mother, but rather despised her for her weakness. For him there was no problem, Dad was right. Eve, his older sister, became the 'good' girl who looked after the younger children, did the shopping and never stopped worrying about her frail, depressed mother whom she felt she had to 'mother'; she was a ten-year-old child without a childhood.

Symptoms found in children which are a reaction to domestic violence may also be found in those who have to deal with the separation of their parents: physical responses, especially problems with sleeping, are frequently cited and many children are anxious and withdrawn, sometimes to the extent of feeling life is not worth living. Very young children show distress by a failure to thrive, which can be an indication of their unhappiness for other reasons, but the possibility of violence, whether threatened, witnessed or suffered, should not be overlooked.

A violent man may want to believe that if a child does not see the violence then no harm is done. He might send his child into another room or upstairs in the belief that if she can't see then she won't hear either. If you are a small child sitting at the top of the stairs, petrified with fear, you hear very well. Even if you are too young to go to school you are not too young to be aware of the anger and hate and the potential danger presented by a grown man out of control, and of your mother bleeding and battered. You become adept at crying silently. Nearly all the children in one North American study could give detailed accounts of the violence, something of which parents were unaware (Jaffe et al. 1990), and this observation I can confirm from personal knowledge.

## Children Who Don't Appear to React

Sometimes children appear to ignore the situation, leaving the adults to sort it out themselves: if they intervene, their fears for their own physical safety or of making a bad situation worse are too often soundly based. But it is possible that there are children who are genuinely not emotionally involved. In this connection some Canadian research found that about a quarter of children who came from families with domestic violence were not affected by it and two-thirds of the boys and four-fifths of the girls were within 'normal' limits of functioning (Wolfe et al. 1985). The implication of this research is that living in a stressful environment does not always result in emotional damage. This study also found that the chance of recovery for all children was high if the violence stopped and support was available.

## The Effect of Negative Experiences

Research in this field commonly focuses on negatives, but among the many influences which affect a growing child will be positive experiences. What are the factors which help a child to endure a childhood of fear and violence? Obviously, those whose mothers survive well and whose mothers have supportive family and friends are likely themselves to have personalities which are not overwhelmed by bad situations and are likely to have found support or areas of success outside the family. It is probable that children with some or all of these characteristics are less likely to experience long-term negative consequences. But, without losing sight of the fact that domestic violence is common amongst all segments of society, domestic violence is often one component contributing to a stressful childhood, rather than a separate cause of a negative outcome. Bad experiences, as well as good ones, are cumulative.

Unhappy children can have emotional problems, including being fearful or withdrawn, being depressed, having poor social skills or demonstrating psychosomatic symptoms. Young children may not develop well: their milestones are delayed and they appear listless and unhappy. Older children become rebellious and aggressive and progress at school is poor. Without some knowledge of the family it is difficult to know the reasons for these symptoms. The sense of having so little power, and the self-given responsibility to protect and care for the more vulnerable parent alluded to earlier, can also be present for these children whose basic needs, especially for stability and security, nurture and care, are in jeopardy. Are they reacting to living in a hostile environment, to separating parents, to long-term inadequate parenting skills, or is domestic violence the key to understanding their unhappiness?

## Domestic Violence and Contact

What children hope for most does not often happen immediately; as has already been said, domestic violence does not always end when parents separate. Hurt and anger can be stronger than reason and unfortunately the difficulties of making contact arrangements for the children when feelings are running so high mean that all too often the children are caught in the middle of the hostility.

The thinking at present is that, with very few exceptions, children benefit from having a continuing relationship with their fathers; and certainly for the majority this cannot be disputed. Nevertheless, if domestic violence is or has been present, the desirability of the father having contact with his children ought to be questioned. This would involve having some knowledge of the history of the family – something not currently considered appropriate or necessary in mediation meetings, where the emphasis is on the present and the future (see Chapter 12). Where there is the possibility of risk to the children arrangements can be made for fathers to see them in a neutral setting such as a Contact Centre, but in many areas it can only be used for a limited period and is in any case a solution which many fathers are not comfortable with. Nevertheless, it does mean they are able to see their children for a short while during which other adults involved know the children are in a safe environment. Children who wish to see their father know that in a Contact Centre they will be safe.

Those children exposed to domestic violence vary in their response to it. Some do not want any contact with the father and say so very firmly; they have lost all love and respect for what he has done to them and to their mother. In other circumstances more thought needs to be given if the right decision is to be reached. Perhaps, as one study suggested, it is the stress which the domestic violence causes to the mothers that is particularly damaging for children, rather than the violence itself (Wolfe et al. 1985). The implication of this research is that a child might continue to feel that she must protect the mother after the father has left and this can provide the main reason for her wanting to sever the links with him.

Seven-year-old Craig lived with his parents and younger sister. He had witnessed many episodes of his father's violence towards his mother, including incidents when she had been thrown downstairs and made a number of visits to the hospital for broken bones. Mother and children were deprived of food, forced to sleep in one room and could only leave the house when it was absolutely necessary. The children knew that if they disobeyed it would be their mother who would be hurt, not themselves. A neighbour gave Craig's mother the phone number of the Women's Aid Federation as the first step to their finding safety in a women's refuge. Craig described his fear that when they did finally leave, his father would follow them, a fear which changed to joy when they had arrived safely undetected. Their relief, though, was short-lived as the father wanted contact with his two fearful children, maintaining in truth that he had not hit them violently. In this instance the court was influenced by the children's unequivocal wish not to see their father and decreed that their wishes should prevail; the father's application for direct contact with them was refused and in time Craig and his sister were able to make a good recovery.

In not a few instances children who experience domestic violence definitely do want to continue their relationship with their fathers. They have no doubt that their love for him is greater than the fear his behaviour has caused and they would feel bereft if they could not see him. Certainly, if a father is aggressive to his partner but is deeply loved by his child then it does seem to be in the child's best interests to maintain contact with him providing the child's safety is a paramount consideration. Family Centres help but do not cover all geographical areas and may be a considerable distance away; an alternative is for the meetings to take place where other people are present, such as in the house of a relative.

Although the court must take into account the wishes and feelings of the child it is quite difficult, if not impossible, for children to tell a court officer, even after two or three meetings, what they really feel because of the fear of unknown consequences or because their loyalty for both parents is too strong.

The words of an eight-year-old hinted at another reason why in such complex situations a child's views may be hard to discover: 'Nobody asks me what I want, they just tell me what to do.' To have a new experience of making such an important decision to a stranger can be very worrying. Information from refuges confirms this; children usually take a long time before they feel safe enough to disclose abuse which is likely to be hard to speak about given the child's tangled web of emotions. It is to be hoped that before long the present practice in England of not hearing children's views, not providing the best circumstances for them to do so, and often not believing that what they say could be true, will change.

## Loving a Violent Dad

There is a strong argument in situations where a child loves a violent dad and both want to continue the relationship, for the contact arrangement to be for a limited period, perhaps for a given time during which the father can be made aware of ways of relating to children other than by domination or fear. At present many contact arrangements are made soon after the separation but prove not to be always in the best interests of the child. One reason is that they are not flexible and what is appropriate for a young child is not necessarily appropriate for a teenager. Yet the contact arrangements can continue until the child is eighteen because of the expense for the resident parent of returning to court, though in reality the court is not likely to enforce the arrangements long before this time. It is regrettable that at present the law hardly recognizes that children's views and wishes about contact can change, as can those of parents.

Another reason for a possible change in contact arrangements is that abuse could be taking place but is undetected. Unless an official knows what information or clues he or she is looking for, no relevant information will be found. This was brought home to me personally when I retired from working in a Child and Family Clinic. The extent of sexual abuse was little realized until near my retirement when there was more awareness and guidelines were drawn up. On looking through past notes I became aware, with some consternation, that in a small number of files there were signs of abuse which no one had noticed. At the time we simply did not understand the implications of what we were being told by family members.

Many lone mothers sincerely believe that contact between father and child is in the best interests of the child and they do their best to help the relationship to continue; and of course they might welcome a few hours' break from caring for the children. However necessary and beneficial this is for her, the overwhelming need is to keep the children safe from harm and free from parental differences, whether physically or verbally expressed. Experience of seeing parents settling differences by co-operation and not by abusive behaviour provides a very good model for children but is something not many of these children have experienced.

### Children Growing Up

The lack of childhood security caused by domestic violence can still haunt adults, taking away their spontaneity and leaving them anxious or depressed. Other long-term effects of a childhood of fear can be a lack of trust in adults and a belief that deception is an integral part of family life. But there can be increased aggression manifested in violent and uncontrolled behaviour. Warm, caring relationships and a desire to make changes will reduce the risk of emotional problems. Will they be victim or aggressor? Use fear and threats or discussion and compromise? Resort to pain and punishment to control their own children or use the children's desire to please and be approved of? These are difficult problems to sort out without a role model who, for boys, needs to be both strong and caring. And can there be, for them, a loving relationship without fear? Can they be exposed to such an experience on which to model themselves while growing up?

It will be apparent from what has already been said that more knowledge is needed about what happens before and after divorce. A limitation of many studies is that they are not long-term and have no follow-up but such indications as there are show that violence or the threat of violence does more long-term damage to children than the separation itself (Rodgers and Pryor 1998). It is known that many children remain undamaged by their experience, though there is a risk that they might not be as successful as they could be unless they receive support and learn other ways of dealing with differences. For the more fortunate children, the effects of domestic violence, like divorce, need not inevitably last for ever.

It has not been satisfactorily explained just why some children grow up to become antisocial or violent teenagers or aggressive adults, and also to identify those influences which help unloved children avoid the danger of following the path of aggression. Few studies have been conducted into boys who become violent fathers and who have, in consequence, been called 'invisible perpetrators'. Abused girls are thought by some to have learned to be victims as children, and are thought when adult to be attracted to violent men; for them, being a victim is a familiar pattern. This again is a generalization, and ignores the possibility of benign influences that are capable of producing change; and it is often also far from the truth.

### Finding Help

'One in seven of the children who called us with family relationships as their main problem reported physical assaults and one in 30 sexual assaults' (ChildLine 1998, p. 7). This analysis showed that by far the most serious problem for these children was violence by a parent towards them or to the other parent or parent-figure. In that one year, more than 8,000 children called about being physically assaulted and more than 3,500 called about sexual assaults by a parent or parent-figure. Many children, anxious about family conflict, talked about their feelings of rejection and fear of being abandoned. They had become aware of the circumstances in which violence occurred and could relate them to causes; many children repeatedly forgave their parent, explaining that they had a drink problem, a drug addiction or a serious mental health problem. A not inconsiderable number blamed themselves for their parent's behaviour.

In these circumstances some children responded with self-destructive behaviour, or turn on others by bullying; some had run away, while others became depressed. Parents and teachers are often surprised at so many children knowing the telephone number of ChildLine, and even some very young ones know how to dial the police or get help from someone. ChildLine has proved to be a very important resource for these troubled children by providing a service which listens to them, believes what they say and promises to take no action without the child's permission.

Another important source of help for children whose mothers suffer serious violence is the Women's Aid Federation which can provide accommodation for them in a Women's Aid refuge; more than 28,000 children are helped in this way every year. With the growing awareness of the importance of encouraging children to express their feelings, the majority of refuges in England and Wales employ child support workers. In the refuges women feel safe and find help and support to make a new start for themselves and for the children. Similar initiatives have taken place in a number of countries. Refuges in Denmark and North America also employ staff to help children. A Children's Program in America has been established as part of a larger Domestic Abuse Project, which organizes self-help and educational groups for abused women and their children, covering a number of issues such as establishing responsibility for the violence, conflict resolution, protection planning for children in violent situations, expressions of feelings – notably of shame and isolation – gender-role issues, and building self-esteem.

Important work is also being done in Australia, where the Family Law Act 1995 states that the court must consider the need to protect children from the physical and psychological harm of being subjected or exposed to abuse, of ill-treatment, of violence or other behaviour, or of being present while a third person is subjected or exposed to these situations. There was concern about the high number of incidents witnessed by children under five and the number of incidents in which guns were used (Kaye 1996). The Children and Domestic Violence Group, an umbrella organization in Australia, works to eliminate male violence and to promote services for children (Saunders 1995, p. 38).

New Zealand has also addressed the subject with the Guardianship Amendment Act 1995 which states that if violence has been used against a child the court will not give the violent person custody or allow access other than under supervision unless it is satisfied that the children will be safe.

Children fortunate enough to find an adult who can listen sympathetically and whom they can trust, may receive enough support to enable them to deal with the emotional effects of violence which are nearly impossible for an outsider to contemplate. The subject of Chapter 9, helping children, is also relevant to children who are victims of domestic violence.

# 7   Listening to Children

Listening to children over the years talking about their distress at the time of their parents' separation led to my considering how the process could be handled so as to limit the stress or even, as unlikely as this might sound, make a positive experience for children. To this end it seemed important to talk directly to those who did think their parents got it right; this proved more difficult than expected.

Those who were seen were children of friends, colleagues or acquaintances. Despite a local newspaper publishing an article on the matter and my being interviewed by the local radio station, nobody else come forward. It may be there are not many children and young people who feel that although it wasn't perfect, their parents did succeed in making it a good divorce for them. However, there are a number of other possible reasons. As many of the separations had happened some years previously it may be surmised that a number of those who did feel their parents did well are happy with, or resigned to, the situation. To discuss the event much later could remind them of what had been a painful time, even though the outcome was satisfactory, hence their reluctance to risk this happening. Others said they were too young to know a different situation, or have forgotten how they felt, saying their experience was the same as other children's and not interesting. Whatever the reason for the difficulty in finding more young people to interview, those I did talk to confirmed one of the important tenets of this book, that it is possible for parents to ensure that children have a 'good' divorce.

Those who had volunteered to be interviewed, both boys and girls, were told that I was writing a book concerned with the feelings of children and young people about their parents' divorce or separation, and because there seemed to be more emphasis on what parents should not do, and the harm children suffer as a result of the separation, I wanted to talk to some children who thought that their parents had handled the situation as well as possible and, although not perfect, basically the divorce was all right for them.

I proposed a meeting with the children and young people on their own, to last not more than an hour. They would be in charge of the discussion and could choose not to say anything which made them uncomfortable. For my part I promised to keep the information absolutely confidential and not write anything which could identify or link them with what was discussed. The four issues I thought it would be useful to discuss were: how it was before the separation, what happened at the time and just after, what made it all right, and how they feel now about what happened.

I emphasized that what they said could be of benefit to other children whose parents lived apart, and that their views would be especially useful to parents who intend to separate and are concerned to do their best for their children. This prompted the last question, which was to ask what, in their opinion, was the most important thing that couples who had not actually separated could do which would help their children.

No age was stipulated; in fact the youngest was fourteen and the oldest in the twenties. As all but two were teenagers, this is how, for the sake of style, I will refer to them. None of them were well-known to me personally, but they were linked indirectly because I had heard of them through friends and acquaintances. All could be described as articulate, white and middle class. Nevertheless, despite being a very small, self-selected sample of nine from a limited section of society, the common elements in the responses do suggest certain positive steps parents could take to minimize the effects of separation on their children, by considering their responses to the main question: What do parents have to do to get it right for their children?

## What the Children Said

### Feelings Respected, and Honest Communication
A number of the young people expressed the same ideas using different words; I highlight the views most often expressed. The first was a comment made by many to the effect that throughout the process of separation the children's feelings were respected and never forgotten. They were free to ask questions concerning themselves and their opinions were sought over issues which affected them. Two said they had not been told details of the reasons why the couple had separated – which they thought was right; adults' infidelities or shortcomings were not topics they wanted to hear about. A number of them commented on the importance of their questions being answered honestly.

Most but not all of them had been aware of the antagonism between their parents and remembered the growing intensity of the rows. The usual pattern was for the father to leave the family home – an event which left some mothers sad for a while, but for others any distress felt was alleviated by relief based on the belief that this was the right thing for the family.

*Timing*
The timing of the various changes was thought about and the best solutions found. Most parents spaced the changes so that, for instance, Dad leaving, new partners arriving, and having to sell the house happened at different times. The gradual introduction of the major changes was thought helpful, though one teenager felt guilty at the time because the separation had been delayed until she was older, when it was thought it would be easier to accept because it would not coincide with the stress of examinations. This was her reaction after a delay of only a few months; what effect the knowledge that their parents stay together for years 'for the sake of the children' has on the children themselves is hard to imagine.

*Contact With Both Parents*
At the time of the interview all the young people were still in contact with both parents even though the separation had taken place some years previously. Most of them felt that their base was with their resident parent but their relationship with the other parent was still ongoing and they felt comfortable in both houses. The degree of satisfaction this accorded them varied but it was important that they were part of their dad's family, and for some the relationship was such that they could choose not to go if there were other commitments involving their friends.

For an adolescent, flexibility is very important and this was the problem most often mentioned. A number were pulled between doing what they wanted to do, such as going to a party with their friends, or visiting Dad because it was 'his' weekend, and in their opinion not to see him would cause him to be hurt or angry because it reinforced any feeling he might have had of being the least important parent. A difficulty for one teenager, which was subsequently solved, was caused by having a parent who insisted on his weekend; even though the teenager fully understood why, his feeling was that this wasn't a mutual coming together as it took away his freedom to choose whether to see his father or not. Faced with this dilemma, concern for the father's feelings meant that usually the contact visit took place, as arranged. Most of those interviewed indicated that they were aware that other difficulties were common to most young people, whether their parents lived together or not, and were more related to teenager–parent issues than to separated parents.

Several valued the increased number of interested adults in their lives and all of them, to greater or lesser degree, had 'new' people they felt warmly about and by whom the feeling was reciprocated, but the 'old' were also important because of the stability they brought to their lives.

## The Parental Relationship

Comments were made about the parental relationship, with some of the participants saying that they knew their parents could not live together but they still were concerned about one another. One or two were pleased that family members from both sides were friendly – in one family even Mum's ex-husband and her new partner were amicable.

The general expectation in society seems to be that separated parents will continue to have a hostile relationship, whereas the young people interviewed here had parents who felt varying degrees of friendship towards their ex-partner. They therefore felt that their family was different from the majority, something which pleased them as this had been achieved despite society's expectation to the contrary. 'There's no point in parents separating and still continuing the battles', said one participant. The majority said they had either changed or modified their feelings, believing their current situation to be better than living in a house where the adults had rows. They thought that both parents were happier after their separation. More than one thought her parents would not have continued their relationship if they had not had children but, nevertheless, they were involved in family celebrations and had never ceased to be loving, caring parents.

None of them felt used by their parents and a number thought it helped if parents had a supporting network. 'Mum had a number of friends to talk to' was a repeated comment. For a brief period one father tried to get his child to be an advocate for him, but this was not felt to be a serious matter for the young person involved.

The consensus of those with step-parents was that stepfathers and stepmothers who did not take an active part in child-rearing and did not behave as if they were natural parents, but helped when asked and were generally supportive, are appreciated. One said if he were upset he would not expect his mother's partner, a person he had a good relationship with, to comfort him because he knew, and accepted, that in these circumstances it would be Mum's place to do so. It is this sort of start which can – and for a number of these teenagers did – develop into sincere affection on both sides; not parental, but understanding and friendly.

In two of the families the resident parent had been optimistic about the separation: 'It'll be better for all of us, we'll all be much happier' was a sentiment which influenced the children. Those of school age at the time appreciated that they felt all right once they were no longer worried about having to change schools and lose friends.

### Advice to Parents

Advice to parents about to separate was to try to get on together and, if you can't be friends, at least be polite to each other. As children these young people did not have to choose between their parents or be involved in their hostility, but without exception they knew that both parents loved them and were united over their well-being. The arrangement for one child, which she did not recommend, had been to spend one week with her mother and one week with her father. This she accepted when she was young as the relationship between them was good, but later, as a teenager, she found the arrangement irksome. As a result, as soon as she had left school, she left both her homes to live with friends, though she is still in touch with both parents and their new families. Again, it was the lack of hostility between parents which was stressed and which made a continuing warm relationship with both families possible.

In one sentence, their advice to parents was: put your relationship with your child before that of a new partner, certainly at the beginning; don't stop being involved with and interested in your children; make changes gradually; and don't involve children in conflict or marital difficulties. What they said in different ways was that it was their awareness that they were loved by both parents which was more important than anything else. A number commented on the change in the relationship over time; they needed both their parents very much at first but once they became settled and secure they could do what all teenagers do and gradually become independent, a task made very much easier if parents are in the background and remain supportive.

### Related Issues

Each teenager was seen only once, but it is likely that if further interviews had been arranged they may have been more forthcoming about the difficulties because the situation would then not be new to them. Nevertheless listening to them I was struck by their sensitivity and their awareness and concern about their parents' feelings. This, as well as their maturity and optimism, was the overriding impression gained from meeting these young people. They all had great plans for their future and expected to get married and have children, though some of them said they would take a great deal of care over getting to know a partner before making a commitment. As a group they were confident and independent. Obviously they all had parents who considered how they would be affected by any changes and who did their best to minimize the negative effects.

An important aspect of the situation in every instance was that, though there were financial difficulties in a number of the households, they did not have to contend with a much lower standard of living. This would have added to the difficulties in many areas of their lives and produced some deterioration in their quality of life, as it does to many children in that situation. Neither were they school dropouts, delinquents, academic failures, or likely to be amongst society's casualties. To meet them conveyed to me a very powerful message of success; these teenagers were a credit to themselves and the adults involved in their lives. Many of the parents I meet are worried about the effect their divorce will have on their children. If they could hear these teenagers talking, they could not fail to be impressed by the impact of their statements and take heart from them.

My hope was to gain confirmation that divorce for children, in the long term, need not be a negative experience, given the proviso above that the family is not experiencing poverty and the marital war has ceased. That a damaged future will inevitably result for children is the impression conveyed by the media and much of the research on the topic. However, there are indications that this is changing, a topic to be discussed fully in a forthcoming study by Professor Carol Smart of the University of Leeds. Her views are based on interviewing over a hundred children and focusing on shared or co-parenting.

Talking with these teenagers demonstrated to me very vividly that if both parents want a good divorce for their children and they co-operate in their role as parents, then it is perfectly possible to have one. It is how parents react with each other and separately with the children which is crucial for a 'good divorce'.


## THE WORDS OF YOUNGER CHILDREN

The most vivid comments about the effects – quite largely ill-effects – of divorce on the family are those made by the children themselves. Throughout this book they have been interspersed to illustrate various points; here they are amplified and, as always, have had to be disguised in the interests of confidentiality. For most of these younger children the experience is relatively new; they have not reached the stage of being able to look back, a limited number being still in the early stages of distress and experiencing a great deal of anxiety about what will happen, though often such feelings are not simple and straightforward. Some of the comments have been made by children in groups over the last eight years; others come from my work with individual children over a much longer period, and yet others from working with families.

An analysis of the opinions, both written and oral, of fifty-three of these children has been made. It is a random, not a scientific, sample and is intended to convey the feelings children have when they are on their own or with others in groups, feelings which have been kept secret, sometimes for a number of years, until they found a place which was safe where they could be shared without any consequences. It has to be stressed that the material was assembled in retrospect, and had not been collected with any idea of using it at the time the remarks were made.

It is not known how typical the children are; to be seen on their own or to be a member of a group in no way indicates that they are children with problems. Only a small proportion could be described as having an emotional problem but for a number there was not the opportunity to discover whether their difficulties pre-dated the separation, were a response to it or were related to their subsequent experiences. Overall it could be presumed that these children were likely to live with a parent who cared for their welfare and feelings. Most of the comments were from children aged between six and twelve, though a few were teenagers.

### Children Who Love Both Parents

A majority of children expressed a general sadness about their situation; they loved both parents and desperately wanted them together again. As one seven-year-old said, 'I think it is better for mummies and daddies to separate, but it's not better for the children. I like both my parents. I am sad about my mum and dad.' The most frequently expressed wish children had was that Mum and Dad would live together again: 'I wish Mum and Dad were together'; 'I wish they loved each other'; or, 'I wish we could be a family again.' A six-year-old wrote: 'Mum is by best friend. Dad is good fun to be with. Dad is the person who is closest to me. My best wish is for Dad to come home.' And another said he was 'lonely because I don't have anyone to talk to at home'. A lot of their loving contained anxiety; for example, 'I worry about Mummy falling off an aeroplane'; 'I worry about Daddy having an accident'; 'I worry about Mummy being in a fire'; 'I worry about Daddy having a car crash.' One solution to divorce, proposed by an eight-year-old boy, was: 'If Daddy worked all day and Mummy worked all night it would be OK.'

**Fears and Worries**

It would be true to say that for most children there are two main worries which are uppermost in their minds. The first concerns their parents and their safety and welfare, and the second concerns whether they will still be loved no matter what happens. Many of the incidents children talk about belong to a time before the separation, but they still occupy their thoughts. Some of these are the same for both parents, especially both parents continuing to love them whatever the circumstances, and their being safe. There are other worries which include:

• Violence – Dad hitting Mum; the police coming; Dad punching or attempting to strangle the child and Mum; hitting Mum with an object such as a frying pan, a stick or a bat; kicking; throwing Mum down the stairs; Dad trying to take the children away.

• Dad breaking Mum's ornaments; breaking crockery.

• Harsh disciplining – the child being sent to bed without food, or being locked in the bedroom.

• Threats to the child or to the mother.

Worries relating to the mother:

• Whether Mum loves/wants her; Mum putting her new partner first and the child no longer being loved.

• Mum walking out of the house again and maybe not coming back; Mum committing suicide.

• Being a messenger between parents; letting out adult secrets.

• Mum getting married again; Mum not getting married again.

• Mum drinking too much and the child has to care for her; Mum's health; Mum's smoking; Mum's safety; Mum having an accident such as dying in a fire.

• Concern about paying bills.

Worries relating to the father:

- Whether Dad loves/wants the child; Dad has a new partner and maybe a new family and the child fears he is no longer loved; Dad fusses over the new baby and the child fears he has been usurped; Dad hasn't been in touch and the child fears he has forgotten he exists; losing touch with Dad.

- Dad dying; Dad committing suicide.

- Dad drinking and the child's worries that when Dad drives the car he might have an accident; Dad's smoking; Dad dying in a plane accident.

- Having to live with Dad; Dad wanting the child to stay overnight when the child doesn't want to; Dad breaking promises.

- Dad not giving Mum money for the children's keep because he is mean; Dad trying to kidnap the child from school and the school threatening to call the police.

- The possibility that Dad will be lonely or won't manage well alone.

One wrote about another worry: 'The most difficult thing is for me to keep Dad's secrets.'


**Their Relationship With Their Father**

Nearly half of the children made positive comments about their father. This does not mean there were not others who also felt positive, but I know that these did so. Neither does it mean that perhaps in a year's time a number of them who currently want to see their father might have a different view if they are being treated in a harmful way. These children said they loved Dad, missed him and worried about him. Others wanted him home while accepting that if this happened the rows would continue, though this was in fact a dilemma which none had to face. Some did see their father but would have liked the meetings to be more frequent. Sentiments such as 'He's nice; you can talk to him' were frequently expressed. 'Mummy is nice, but Daddy is very, very nice', said one small boy.

These children missed their fathers very much. Some blamed themselves either for the break-up itself or because they could not do anything to stop it happening. 'I feel so helpless because there is nothing I can do to bring them together', was the feeling expressed by a number of them. Another anxiety was that if they did not see Dad he might think it was because they did not love him any more. In reality the opposite was more likely to be true; it was Dad who was most likely to break the contact. Some don't stop loving either parent, however badly they have been treated; for example, 'I love Daddy very much although he is not a good man', or, 'After all, he is my dad.'

Fewer children were negative about their father, with rather less than a quarter in this sample saying that they hated him and never wanted to see him again. Two of them wanted to see him less often than they did. There is, of course, the possibility that some of these views would change over time, as a parent's view of his or her child tends to change when he or she gets to know the child without the other parent being present; but this was not a matter considered when the material was collected. One seven-year-old said she had been very worried when Mum and Dad had fights and was relieved when her dad moved out. Now she was afraid of going to Dad's house but Mum said she had to go. The children's anger at and fear of their father sometimes related to his behaviour in the past – especially if they had experienced or witnessed violence – or to his present actions. Children quite often used the groups to share the trauma of past episodes with others who, sadly, knew all too well what they were talking about.

Four children talked about their father attempting to take them out of school or of threatening to do so, and a number were hit. One child was upset, not because her dad hit her but because he hit her three-year-old brother 'very hard'. Dads can't be trusted, they tell lies and don't keep promises, were the experiences of at least five of the children.

Amongst this group were children who did not want to see their father because they felt rejected or unwanted. Fathers whose current behaviour upset their children included those who criticized and made nasty remarks to the children or abused them emotionally in some way. 'He hurts my feelings' was the response of more than one child. Some of the comments reported by the children concerned actions and words which did not amount to physical abuse and could hardly be called emotional abuse but nevertheless left deep and long-lasting scars. One father's nickname for his daughter throughout her child-hood was 'Useless'. 'Why did I have to have such an ugly child as you?' was the sort of comment he would make to her.

Another father gave away his son's train set without saying anything to the child. When the little boy asked him about it, he said: 'Well you didn't play with it very often and I had to do the man who had it a favour.' He had no idea that for this boy the train represented good memories of a happier time and was used in his imaginative play as an escape route from his present, near-intolerable situation. A number of children told stories of their parent's utter unawareness of their feelings 'My dad doesn't think I feel anything,' said one, 'he says it is because I am just a child.' Another said, 'I tell Dad he upsets me when he says bad things about Mum but he just laughs and goes on doing it.' Those who listen to children know that they are deeply upset by such unkindness; this hurt can last a lifetime.

These children no longer felt that Dad saw them as 'special'. Sometimes this was because he preferred his new partner or her children – a situation made worse if the child believed that he was not really wanted except as a weapon to be used in the continuation of the marital battle. A few said they were frightened of their father because he was violent to them, he made threats or made them anxious by making critical remarks about their mother. Three of the children said their fathers told them repeatedly that Mummy was bad and one day the court would let the children live with him. This causes uncertainty, worry and confusion, especially if Mummy is loved and Daddy is feared. Five had vivid memories of violent episodes they had witnessed when parents were together, a few having experienced the safety of a refuge.

### Their Relationship With Their Mother

About a third of the children expressed positive feelings, though many more talked of affectionate feelings for their mother which were not recorded verbatim. In the groups, mothers were mentioned less than fathers, who were more often talked about because, being absent, they were the ones who aroused a greater variety of emotions; it was not that mothers were thought less of. Mums were there, doing what mums always do; perhaps warm feelings about her did not have to be stated. They talked about feeling close to her and worrying about how she was managing. 'I worry about her; she is the one that really matters to me.' A fear mentioned a number of times was that she might also go away, a fear so strong as to make it difficult for them to concentrate on other things. Would she be home when they returned from school or from seeing Dad? 'Mum is lovely; I know she will never leave me', was a sad comment because it implied this was a worry for the child.

A much smaller number made negative remarks about their mother. Amongst these six children were those who blamed her for the separation – it was her fault Dad had left. Others resented how they were being treated. These included those who were being brought up without any demonstration of affection or worth and those who were punished with severity. One child, who had had a very hostile relationship with his mother for some time, was, as a consequence of counselling, able to share his feelings with her. This produced a greater understanding and a significant improvement in their relationship. Unfortunately, some are rejected by their mother, perhaps because they are a reminder of past failures, or perhaps because the mother resents the affection the child has for his dad.

## Some General Comments

Ten children expressed ambivalent feelings about their parents, especially their fathers: 'I love him but I am frightened of him'; 'I love him but I am angry with him too because I don't think he loves me'; 'I am not sure whether Daddy loves me or not'; 'I love Mummy but she likes my little sister best.' One child said that she did not want to see her daddy. No, that was wrong, she wanted to see him but wished she didn't have to because it was too hard.

Children also made some general comments about parents. A number were worried that one or other parent drank too much; ten of them talked of the rows between their parents continuing, despite the separation. If the child was aware that the hostility concerned contact visits and therefore themselves, and was conducted in their presence, then it was very painful. The one thing they thought would improve with separation, the frightening rows, was as bad as it had ever been and could be worse if, as some children said, they were involved in the arguments at the beginning and end of contact visits.

As has been pointed out in several contexts, a considerable number said that they were upset by not being told what was happening. A ten-year-old said: 'Why don't they tell me honestly? I'm not stupid and I need to know where I'm going to live and whether I shall have to move school. Neither Mum nor Dad will talk to me about what is going to happen. I'm fed up with their lies.'

About half the children with step-parents were happy with their present situation, the other half not; mainly because they felt left out or found having the children of the partner difficult to contend with. Teenagers, particularly, felt they needed privacy, away from younger children.

Other worries concerned the future. Would Dad want to see them when they were adult? One wrote: 'I worry that I will never be able to see my dad when I am a grown-up.' Others ask: 'Will Mum or Dad stop loving me when they get married again?'; 'Will I get married and be happy?'; 'Does divorce run in families?'; 'Will my children go through my pain?'

Six of the children said they were bullied at school and teased because 'Your dad doesn't live at home.' This may be an expression of how they saw themselves. If, in their eyes, Dad has rejected them, then the expectation was that everyone else would too. Often they talked about the difficulty of making friends and the feeling that they were different from other children – this perhaps involved an element of envy of the others, though this was difficult to admit, but certainly they felt inferior. They had lost their sparkle, their zest for life, which had made them less interesting for other children to be with. Too often such depression drives away children and teachers alike.

These children are basically dealing with a trauma which quite often has taken over their thoughts temporarily. The picture gained from those who feel safe enough to express their fears and anxieties, knowing there will be no consequences which they cannot control, is one of anxious children with many worries who are deeply concerned about their parents. Five described how they parented their parent, solicitously taking on duties willingly. A five-year-old said: 'Mummy cries a lot so I make her a drink.' A nine-year-old told a group: 'Mum tried to talk to a friend but it wasn't any help because the friend didn't understand, but she knows I do so she tells me.' Fortunately, with time parents become emotionally stronger and take charge of their lives.

Without doubt, some of the anxieties could be alleviated by parents sharing more information with the children which concerns them and by asking for their opinion. Nine of the children made comments such as: 'Nobody told me what was happening. I felt left out.' 'I didn't want to decide between Mum and Dad but I wish they had asked me what I thought.'

What a number of children have found is that their views changed with time. When separation first happens most are broken-hearted, but when they are told honestly what is taking place and that they still have two caring parents they become more resigned to the situation. They begin to be aware that there are positives: for instance, the rows become less terrible and less frequent, they enjoy having two Christmases (if this is not a source of parental friction) and they see both parents who demonstrate their love and approval of them. Then, in time, they manage well and can say, in truth, that the divorce has been better for everyone.

# 8 Children in Groups

## Why Groups?

The focus of this chapter is on groups because these appear to be a comparatively new way of dealing with children in the context of divorce. Their purpose is to provide a setting where children feel safe enough to talk freely about how they felt about their parents' separation and their presents concerns. The children come voluntarily and know that what takes place is not shared with anyone outside the group, and that no action will follow and no decisions will be made. Running groups for children, as described here, has been developed in a very personal way by my fellow worker Branwen Lucas and myself. There are other ways, just as valid, which equally well provide an opportunity for children to share their feelings without repercussions.

## The Legal Background

Two important documents provide legal and philosophical justification for groups. The first is the UN Convention on the Rights of the Child, signed by Britain in 1991, which states two broad propositions concerning children generally and those of divorce: that children have a right to express their views and be listened to carefully on all matters which affect them (Article 12); and that when adults or organizations make decisions which affect children they must always think first about what would be best for the child (Article 3). The UN Convention applies to all signatory states; the English laws are mentioned here and in Chapter 11 not so much for their insular importance but because they involve considerations that are generally applicable.

The second document of significance is the Children Act 1989 which lays down the principle that a child's welfare is paramount and that the Court must pay particular attention to children's wishes and feelings, although there could be some exceptions. The court also has a duty to protect and promote the welfare of children.

## Children's Groups

In the groups the children find support and understanding, and also the opportunity to help one another. 'It's all right to cry here', one eight-year-old told another who was holding back tears when describing a particularly painful experience. It cannot be stressed too strongly that when children are given the opportunity to speak freely, unconcerned by the outcome of what they say – and that is absolutely crucial – they share facts, ideas and feelings in a way that would not be possible for them in any other circumstances. When they talk to other children in the group they do not have to consider what their listeners want to hear, and neither do they have to worry about being disloyal to either parent.

Groups provide the opportunity for them to share their thoughts and to talk about events which sometimes happened a number of years previously but still pervade their thoughts. This might be an incident involving violence or a very hurtful experience of rejection. Andrea told the group a number of times about the time her dad, accompanied by his latest girlfriend, had passed her in the street, pretending not to see her. In one group session she was encouraged to role-play the event, then, using a large doll, she punched and kicked it to demonstrate what she would like to do to the girlfriend. To share this hurtful experience and the resulting anger with a sympathetic group was a cathartic act because it brought her feelings into the open in a different way from merely talking about what had happened.

For those endeavouring to help children in this situation their religious, cultural, linguistic and, most obviously, racial background are occasionally important and have to be respected when appropriate.

Once the children accept that what they say will not be repeated, they feel it is safe to reveal some of their distress in front of their peers. It is an experience enabling many to find relief. 'It's great to find other kids who have been through the same things as me. Nobody who hasn't could begin to understand', and 'After the first time I felt I was floating on air' – these are two of many children's comments which expressed this relief. Some, though, are more comfortable on their own, especially if they feel their experience is very different and their problems are more complex than those of other children.

The emphasis throughout is on the child's feelings, and one message to the child is that it is all right to feel like you do, whether you are angry or sad or confused or anxious, and maybe all of these at different times. It's all right to cry, but find the right time and place. Emily was taking a long time to come to terms with her dad leaving; as she told the group, at school she cried 'every day', but also was upset because she was being bullied. She was encouraged to link the two. It was not suggested that she should try to relinquish her sadness before she was ready, but rather to leave it behind when she went to school. She had been hoping children at school would feel sorry for her and comfort her, but instead they were angry, adding to her sense of isolation. For this ten-year-old the message was that sadness belongs at home and it's OK to start enjoying school again.

A second message is that it's all right to express anger but you have to find ways which don't hurt anybody or anything. It's all right to ask for things which are important to you but if you are not being successful in getting them perhaps you have to learn not to shout, threaten or plead but to remain calm and confident. In other words, if it is not working, try something different, because there is probably a better way of handling the situation. Children are aware that their power has limits – they cannot make Mum and Dad live together, for instance, but they are not powerless and they may be able to make some changes.

## Who Can Join?

What follows describes one way of running a children's group in a mediation centre. Children are referred from many different sources; some have parents who have attended mediation meetings or a parent group at the mediation centre, others are referred by GPs, schools, the courts, court welfare officers and social services. Many parents have a child who has been to a previous group who recommends it to his sibling; others know a child who attended one. Any child aged between six and sixteen whose parents are in the process of divorcing or separating is welcome to attend – the child does not have to have a problem.

## Organization

The groups are held on four consecutive weeks after school and are fairly small, usually no more than six children in a group. Holding group meetings in schooltime has been considered on the grounds that they are comparable to visits to the dentist or doctor. There are disadvantages, though, notably the risk of being conspicuous. Despite the large numbers of children with separated parents, many feel it is a private matter to be shared with a few friends only, if that is possible.

Depending on the number of children, there could be either one or two group leaders in charge. The children, who are roughly the same age, come because they want to, having read a leaflet informing them about the groups. They like the idea of meeting other children who have had similar experiences to their own, and welcome the opportunity to talk and be listened to. The groups are about feelings, but also – and this is an important aspect of them – fun.

## The Sessions

Meetings last an hour and a quarter and start with a drink and biscuits. The first meeting is concerned with getting to know each other and with helping the children to understand the purpose and aims of the groups.

Leaders will empathize with the children's initial anxiety by saying that because they are doing something which is quite new for them, they are probably feeling worried and wondering what is going to happen. This is followed by an explanation of our reasons for running groups. They are told that all feelings are acceptable and the purpose is to share them. They might make new friends, and by the end we hope they will feel less isolated and will have helped themselves and each other. The only rule is that they mustn't hurt themselves or other children, or damage things in the room.

An important part of this first session follows, which is to explain to the children that we, the group leaders, promise we will not tell anybody what is said, including any parent or court or official, and that parents understand this. Neither do we make notes or write reports and the only exception to our not telling is the proviso concerning their safety. We would like everyone to promise that they will keep other children's secrets, though of course they are free to tell anyone what they themselves say. We all solemnly hold hands and make our promise to the group. This is an important start and very necessary if children are going to trust us. In one meeting when confidentiality was being discussed, a child said to a group leader 'Don't you really tell anyone?' No. 'Not even your mum?' No. 'Coo.'

This first session will include exercises designed to help children to relax and begin to trust, a necessary preliminary before the children can feel safe enough to share the worries which plague them and the feelings which fill their minds, especially their sadness and anger. Among the activities might be making labels with their name on, and listing four things they share in their lives, and four things which are different. In this way they find out about each other and in the ensuing discussion begin to share something of their life and feelings. Quite often we produce the outline of a house drawn on a large piece of paper. We suggest that they work together and use the felt-tipped pens to make it their house. This helps the group to bond and also can lead to a great deal of sharing and enjoyment.

How effective these activities can be in binding children and leaders into a harmonious group became clear in one early session when a small girl asked a group leader if her parents were divorced. When told they weren't, the next question was: 'Then why are you in the group?' The expression on the child's face as she realized what she had said, before covering her face as she laughed, was wonderful.

The second session will comprise activities which involve sharing feelings. We might draw a pie-chart, the top of a cake, and ask the children to divide it up according to the strength of their feelings – sad, angry, lonely, confused, fear and OK. All such activities will be discussed with the children: 'You made "lonely" a big slice; I wonder if you could tell us about when you are most lonely?' Alternatively a soft ball is thrown and the one who catches it answers a question from our pile of cards. Some of the questions are emotive: 'Mum and Dad argue about me even though they are divorced; I hate it but what can I do about it?'; 'When I visit Dad he doesn't appear to care and spends the time mending his car. I feel so unhappy. Do I have to go on visiting him?'; 'I think Mum prefers the new baby to me because she never says anything nice to me or gives me a hug any more. What can I do?'; 'How can I cope with being part of two families?' We have to watch the level of anxiety and be ready to relieve it if it should be necessary. Others are straightforward: 'Tell us about something you remember that happened when you were a baby.' Playing Agony Aunts, where one child reads out the same sort of questions from pre-selected cards for the group to discuss, is a variation of this exercise.

Another activity is for them to mime an emotion and have the others guess what is being depicted. Some groups enjoy this kind of acting; it provides an opportunity for them to discuss their own (and other people's) feelings.

Sitting at the table drawing or filling in play sheets are other means to the same end. Families, memories, dreams, scary things, when Mum and Dad were together, and other topics which are relevant to each particular group might be drawn and some use is made of the play sheets developed by the group leaders from those of Don Clark (1989). For example, the children are presented with the outline of twelve faces each depicting a feeling. They are asked to choose two or three to fill in, or colour, and then tell the group why they have chosen those particular faces. The work of the Israeli authors, Ayalon and Flasher, (1993) is a rich source of ideas for this kind of work.

A more recent innovation is the special hat, a splendid dark-blue velvet magician's hat which is put on by anyone who has something important to say. The leaders also put it on from time to time and this strengthens the children's feeling that what they say really matters. One striking and perceptive example from a seven-year-old boy while wearing the hat was: 'I don't think children are to blame. When parents divorce they usually have had lots of rows which get worse and worse until they divorce.'

Anger is the topic for the third week, using a number of different ways to enable the feeling to be expressed. Most enjoy writing angry words on a piece of paper, tearing it up into little pieces and throwing them into a basket; and in this session children never fail to enjoy bashing a large stuffed animal.

To end each of the first three sessions one of the leaders reads a brief extract from a story about two children whose parents quarrel and separate; it is one she has written herself because we have not found one suitable for our purpose. She ends with the question: 'And what do you think happened next?' The children's suggestions are incorporated into the following week's story. Not surprisingly, not many of the stories end on a happy note.

The theme of the last session is looking forward. This can be achieved by the children thinking about the positives in their situation and considering how much their feelings have changed since they received the initial thunderbolt of hearing that their parents were going to separate. The children might act out personal situations they find particularly difficult. One such situation might be telling a parent that they will no longer keep confidences between them. One extreme case was of a father who told his child that she had a half-sister, a child by his girlfriend, but she mustn't tell her mother. The children, each encouraged by the others, might take turns in role-playing situations which they find difficult, such as telling parents that they will no longer listen to one parent saying bad things about the other. In doing so they use their new-found confidence to improve the situation. One boy, when a particular response was suggested, said that it wouldn't be possible to say such a thing to his dad until he could run much faster than he could at the present. But perhaps a seed had been sown and one day it might be possible after all.

We finish by discussing what the children felt about the group. We might ask what they enjoyed or found most helpful and whether they have been able to make some changes or can see things differently now. We hope they feel better about their parents' separation and perhaps understand a little how they, their parents, might have felt. We thank them for coming and sharing their feelings, and want them to know that by doing so they have helped other children.

For the last ten minutes parents are invited to join us and, after reiterating our confidentiality rule, we thank them for bringing the children and ask if they have any questions to ask us. Parents and children are told that the children would be very welcome to join another group at a later date. One group's reaction to this was: 'We'll come tomorrow.' We are aware that four sessions is often not long enough, but at present this is all that can be offered. To have a gap in time has its advantages because children's views change, as do adults', and the gap gives a child time for reflection. In addition they are told that if a child is having a worrying time it would be possible to talk to one of the leaders alone, without waiting. We stress that all children need parents who care for them and obviously these are children who are cared for – otherwise their parent wouldn't be present.

The focus of each session is planned, but this does not mean the programme is set; in fact, it varies with each group and with the different ages of the children and is quite largely child-led. In some groups the children are very active, while others prefer to spend a greater part of the time talking. Flexibility is therefore important; the plan of one group's session may be the same as another's but in practice children respond to one activity but not to another, which is then quickly changed. However, the children are encouraged to find different ways of reacting to familiar situations or to ask for what they want directly – 'I don't want to see Dad every weekend', for example. Or we may discuss a very common problem which the children in the group share, such as a child being upset at school because other children don't like her or she is bullied.

Groups for older children can be different. Teenagers are often more comfortable talking and reflecting on what has happened. Their concerns will include thoughts about themselves as adults. Will they have a happy marriage? Is it worth having a family if there is any risk of their children having to go through the experience of separating parents and all the painful feelings they have had to deal with?

The child's good recovery from divorcing parents depends on a number of factors such as the security he feels in the new situation, and the ending of conflict between parents. The hope is that groups provide a good experience from outside the family to help recovery. Activities are also intended to reinforce the notion that there are some good things about divorce and children should not use it as an excuse for not doing what they want to do. Also, they have coped with a great deal and, given time, things will get better.

## Discussion

By providing an amalgam of enjoyable activities and serious thought, children can, by sharing, free themselves from some of the past pain. Occasionally a child is not ready to share feelings and benefits from being seen alone. One very lively boy found a group with its combination of informality and structure very difficult to deal with, but when he returned fifteen months later and joined another group he was both sensible and sensitive.

There can be problems. Groups are labour intensive, and although the cost of equipment is small it does require a fairly large room with few distractions, such as toys around which are not being used, or evidence that other children have used the room. Arranging for children to attend can also be problematic; they come from widely scattered places in the county making the cost of transport for single parents on a low budget very difficult. Some have to wait because there are not enough children of a similar age to form a new group.

A further point relates to a serious lack of provision for the under-fives. These children are probably more in need of help than others. So far this is a problem we have not tackled because a different solution is needed. A parallel group for lone parents running at the same time is one possibility, provided the rooms and personnel are available.

Not all children appear to get a great deal from the groups; experience has taught some that, whatever the circumstances, adults cannot be trusted. For others, one way to deal with grieving is to be defiant, noisy and active. Some of the younger boys who are not ready to take advantage of the opportunity of sharing feelings prefer to use the time to indulge in robust play. They find sitting down and concentrating just too difficult. Mixing boys and girls sometimes creates problems because of their different levels of maturity, but in other groups some boys show a great deal of understanding and are thoughtful and wise. Ideally it is better for children from the same family to attend different groups, but this is not always possible; an alternative has been to run groups just with siblings, perhaps from two or three families. A group which, unknown beforehand to the leaders, had included two friends was not successful. Children who cannot fit in, for whatever reason, are offered individual counselling which can be, and usually is, more helpful to them.

Amongst the children, both boys and girls, who appear to benefit more than others are those who are aware of other people's feelings and reactions and welcome the opportunity of 'thinking out loud', especially if they do not have anyone they can trust from outside the family to talk to. For others it is the experience of being listened to and having what they say valued, which is important. Repeatedly children say: 'Nobody told me what was going on', or, 'Nobody asked what I thought.'

All are encouraged to think about any possible gains which could result from having separated parents; when they discuss this it is fewer parental rows which children mention most often. Having other people interested in different activities – and in them – can also be a bonus when a parent has a new partner. On the whole children who come to groups are independent, and many of them are very caring, showing great concern for their parents.

In the view of the group leaders the groups do help many children to come to terms with their situation and the children's responses confirm this: 'I felt so alone and now I don't any more'; 'I didn't know I could feel so different.' They begin see their position more positively and they can and do benefit from being able to express feelings in a way which does no harm. Other gains can include a growth in confidence, particularly when it is shown by their ability to ask for what they want in a way which is likely to be successful. Groups may also have helped if children have been freed from their anxieties and want to be involved again in age-appropriate interests and activities. There can be no serious doubt that groups provide a valuable service for many of the children involved. As one mother said: 'She's her old self again; it's wonderful.'

## Group Leaders

Perhaps the most important element in running groups is a rapport between the leaders. It is essential to have a colleague who is sensitive to the nuances of the children's behaviour and speech, who understands group dynamics and who knows when to lead and when to follow. For part of the time during most sessions the information children share can be intensely moving, the distress intense; the group leaders have to be attuned to these moments and deal with the emotions evoked with empathy. It can happen that one leader, perhaps for personal reasons of which she might be unaware, is temporarily lost; but through working together and building mutual trust and respect, each has an unspoken awareness of when the other is in need of assistance and will take over briefly. Both empathize with the children and with each other.

A rapport with children is self-evidently necessary, especially the imagination to develop activities which appeal to different age groups. A large part of this is to enjoy the children, to be pleased with their progress and to convey the sense that everything about them is important – what they think, what they say, what they do. While doing this, though, and however enjoyable the activities are, a group leader must always remember the underlying purpose – to provide an environment where children feel safe enough to share their feelings.

With experience, techniques have changed; less reliance is put on aids such as finger painting, making masks, and equipment such as toy cars and play people. Now there is a higher proportion of talking compared with doing, though they are often used together. As mentioned already, much of what we use has been adapted or devised by ourselves, for example, the story we read is our own, some of the play sheets have been adapted from published ones and others are original, and the different ways the children are encouraged to express anger are constantly being modified.

Experience has taught us a number of things, one being that at the first session, once children really trust the leaders and accept that they will not tell anyone what they say, there is a risk that they will share a great deal that has been bottled up for perhaps a long time. It has been found necessary at the first meeting to make sure this does not happen, otherwise at home the child can regret sharing so much so early and may then be reluctant to return for the next session.

## Knowledge

Leading a group or counselling children individually needs certain basic knowledge. Familiarity with child development, notably the scope and limits of children's understanding and how they express their feelings at different ages, is essential. Children of three or four won't have a clear concept of time, so 'In the new year' does not mean much; children of six or seven might be unclear of the meaning of 'divorce' or 'contact' and at this age won't have completely given up a belief in magic; and those three or four years older have a greater repertoire of ways of exhibiting distress. Teenagers have to come to terms not only with the separation but also with their own feelings of being part-child, part-adult.

Divorce can be akin to the death of a parent, often not as deeply sad, but more complicated because of the feelings of being abandoned or rejected, and the anxiety about being replaced by other adults or children. One ten-year-old shared with the group his grief over the death of his sister, which occurred a few days before his father left. This brave child concluded that whilst both events were deeply painful, at least he could see his father again.

An awareness of the effects of bereavement and the psychosomatic symptoms relating to loss are useful in helping children to deal with another kind of loss, that of a familiar family unit in which both parents, in the child's eyes, belonged (Jewett 1997).

# 9 Other Ways of Helping

Provision for helping children whose parents are separated can be divided into two broad groups. One group, which usually triggers some action and will not be discussed in detail, includes court welfare officers, guardians *ad litem*, and social services officers who are concerned when children are at risk of harm.

Court welfare officers are more involved with the children of divorcing parents than other services. If, prior to obtaining a divorce, there is controversy over issues such as where the child should live or when and how often he should see the non-resident parent, the judge will order a court welfare officer to write a report to assist in making a decision on behalf of the parents. The court welfare officers are empowered to see the child alone and with both parents separately, and also to interview those who know him; for example, members of the child's family, school staff or child-minders. Children know that the person interviewing them will write a report based on what he or she has been told. The purpose is to tell the court something of the child's background, rather than to help the children, though of course this can and often does happen, and to contribute to finding the best solution to issues which cannot be agreed between the parents.

The second group comprises those organizations which are designed to listen to children in confidence with the aim of helping them share the confusion and hurt resulting from what has happened to them. They include a variety of counselling services, Child and Family Clinics, ChildLine and groups for children. A few mediation units offer individual counselling. Some school counsellors, though not all, would be in this group; excluded are those who are obliged to share information with the head teacher. In addition there are some small-scale voluntary groups which do valuable work helping children with their feelings, including Gingerbread. Those who come in contact with families, such as health visitors and doctors, may also contribute to good effect.

## Confidential Services

The children's views will be treated confidentially by this second group, whose members are not usually expected to make decisions or disclose what has been said. The only exception, a universal one, is that if a child discloses ongoing harm or abuse the interview has to be stopped and the matter reported. For the most part, they provide a safe and caring place where children, whether on their own or in groups, can talk about their feelings and be listened to.

ChildLine is different because the children who telephone can remain anonymous if they choose and only with their permission can the counsellor act on the child's behalf. This is an important resource where children can share their feelings of loss or anxiety about parental conflict, as well as the other feelings and problems they have at the time of separation. In the year up to the end of March 1997 over 1,700 children called ChildLine specifically to talk about the effects on them of their parents separating or divorcing; a further 4,500 called about other difficulties which included divorce or separation. In total more than 6,000 children were sufficiently affected by anxieties regarding their parents' break-up to ring ChildLine – this, in a single year.

Different strategies for helping have different aims. It will be clear from the preceding remarks that a number of services are designed to enable children to talk about their feelings, though few of them are concerned with those children whose problem is in one specific area, such as coming to terms with their parents' divorce or with managing the consequences in the best way possible for them. Such children do not normally need the kind of help with psychological problems that is provided by, for example, a Child and Family Clinic; they are engrossed either with painful feelings, or in responding to factors in the situation following separation which they find unsatisfactory. As with groups, for those endeavouring to help children in this situation certain precepts need to be borne in mind; for instance, an appreciation of the religious, cultural, linguistic and, most obviously, racial background is occasionally important.

## COUNSELLING INDIVIDUAL CHILDREN

*Why Alone?*

Children talk to someone on their own for a variety of reasons. It may be the practice of the service they have arrived at; they may be seen by a child psychotherapist; or perhaps they have been offered individual counselling in a clinic, at a GP's surgery, or privately. Some whose parents have separated do not want to participate in a group but prefer to talk to an adult alone.

What follows is a description of individual counselling in one mediation centre. As with groups, children come at their parent's request and are reassured that what transpires will not be shared. It is very much a personal view of working with children. There are many other ways of conducting sessions, each one in part dependent on the purpose of the meetings, the needs of the child and the counsellor's personality and experience.

### Different From Counselling?

The person the child sees is usually called a counsellor, a word which can give the wrong impression, even though what takes place is akin to counselling. It is used here in lieu of a more precise term. Counselling in the ordinary sense is concerned with helping people, whether adults or children, to understand how past experiences in different areas of their lives have influenced their present way of perceiving their situation. It may be about difficulties which have not been resolved or about seeing the past in a more positive way so that they can be freed from the emotional residue which intrudes on the present.

Counselling children with separated parents is akin to what is outlined above but is short term and has a far narrower focus. It is concerned solely with a child's feelings about separation, the subsequent situation or whatever aspect of either is causing the child concern. One way of explaining to the children the purpose of the meetings might be: 'I am someone who *listens* to children but does not tell anyone what is said unless I am told a child is being harmed, then I have to. You do not have to say anything that you do not want to share; you choose what you say and you choose whether you want to come again. In all these ways you are in charge.' The key word is 'listens'. The important things for the child are just too painful to be shared until trust develops.

Children whose parents are separated and are being seen alone are not patients in need of therapy. Rather they are offered a private space for a short while and given an opportunity to think aloud about the trauma they have been through. The focus is mainly on the present and what they feel about the present. Where relevant though, past relationships in the child's life are not ignored. Children have to trust that no action will result from the meetings other than the changes they choose to make themselves. Very occasionally they want their parents to be told something which is difficult for them to share and may need help to do so, but this is their decision.

By having a private opportunity to talk about worries and anxieties and, for many, a new experience of being listened to in a non-judgemental way, children may begin to see things differently and gain confidence. In consequence this will influence how they act and thereby achieve the same aims as groups, particularly in enabling them to make direct statements and to see their situation less passively. Talking about feelings which relate to the divorce – especially the key ones: sadness, anger, fear and confusion – is the core of the work. It is not about taking either parent's side; requests for information from solicitors or others involved in the divorce proceedings are always refused. It can be seen as taking the side of the child through sympathetic, active listening. Some children can respond to the request to leave their worries on my table. Comments such as: 'I feel empty of worries' make the effort to provide support and understanding worth while.

## Organization

In practice, the meetings last between fifty and fifty-five minutes depending on the age of the child. Quite often four meetings are planned (sometimes more are offered if it seems appropriate) which take place after school; as with groups, the one rule is that the child is not allowed to hurt anyone, or the equipment. There will have been a brief contact with the child and parent before the sessions start and, as with groups, at the end of the last session the parent will be invited to join the child for a few minutes, though no information derived through counselling is shared.

## Play Techniques

For younger children the counsellor will need to use play techniques to help communication and at times to relieve tension. Some of these can be used with children alone, although some are suitable for children in groups too. Activities for those on their own are based on what has been called the 'third object' (Winnicott 1968); that is, something which child and counsellor focus on together.

At the beginning of my own contact with a child the 'third object' is a box of shells collected from the seashore. The child may be asked to choose a shell which will be himself; this is put in the middle of a sheet of A4 paper. Then he will be encouraged to make a picture of his family, using a different shell for each person. This is a non-threatening way of finding out about how a child perceives his family, and in nearly all instances gives clues about whom he feels close to; whether there is a strong network of caring people; or whether the family pets dominate the picture rather than the human beings. Sometimes Dad is well and truly in the centre, right next to the child, but other children have put him under the table or, in one case, outside the door. Another version of this activity is to provide a large sheet of paper divided into squares measuring about 7 cm. The child is asked to choose one of several small dolls to represent himself, followed by others for family members. The idea is basically the same as using the shells and gives similar pictures of how a child experiences relationships within the family.

Other activities used with young children include playing with toy farm animals which are very useful in providing for the expression of fear or anger. Fences are important in this regard, to separate the gentle animals from the fierce or to make sure the crocodile doesn't escape. In this respect one writer describes a useful technique of using the third person to tell a story or describe a situation (Bannister 1997); 'This little polar bear has got lost in the snow; I wonder who could help him?'; 'These two tigers are fighting very fiercely. Could anything make them stop?' She also describes the technique of dividing the good bits of Mum or Dad from the bad. The bad bits can be crossed out while the good are retained.

'Erik' can be very useful; he is a soft, German doll about 22 cm long, wearing bright colours including a bright red hat which has a floppy crown. I explain that because Erik comes from a foreign country he can't tell anyone what he hears because he doesn't speak English; but there is a lot of space inside his hat and he likes to hear secrets. I invite the child to whisper one of her secrets to him. I don't know what she whispers but it is a way of giving the worry words and putting them outside the child. Modelling with playdoh can be therapeutic for some; especially the destruction of what they have made. Children can get a great deal from listening to a book with a self-explanatory title – *The Huge Bag of Worries* by Ironside (1996). This book is very good for helping even the older children to open their 'huge bag of worries' in order for their worries to be reconsidered and maybe discarded. Games with puppets which children can use to represent people – much as they use animals – also help communication.

Rather older children might be asked to draw their family as it was and as it is now. Some will write a letter to one parent expressing exactly what they would like to say. Making an eight-page book entitled *ME* is enjoyed by some, with each page covering a different aspect, such as my family, who I live with, other people important to me, my house, my pets, my school and my story.

Some children may be content to draw or model whereas others may spend some time practising difficult situations such as telling

Mum and Dad they will no longer discuss one with the other. Behind all the activities and conversations the counsellor will be aware of the need to give the child the feeling that he matters and that although he does not have the power to get what he wishes, which is often for Dad to return home again, he can make some things happen. Children can also be made aware that eventually they can decide it is time to leave the adults to sort out their own problems, while they themselves concentrate, though not consciously, on their own life.

As with groups, anger is sometimes the focus. This is a time when children learn that it is safe to express some of their anger and nobody is upset. An eight-year-old had witnessed a great deal of violence before his father left. His hatred and fear of his dad dominated his thoughts. In this 'angry' session he acted out every torture he could think of in order to make his dad suffer. He pretended he was the grown-up and, using a large teddy bear to represent his father, he shouted at it every obscenity he knew. He threw the toy around the room, his face contorted with rage: 'Just you wait, just you wait', he kept repeating, until finally he collapsed into a chair, saying, 'That was great.' His anger had found a safe place to be expressed and put outside himself and nobody had been harmed.

In play a young child can express disloyalty or frightening rage in ways such as this without fear of the consequences, and can end the sequence in any way he chooses. Older children may be happier talking, but most use pen and paper to write or draw in order to clarify their thoughts.

The emphasis throughout is on feelings. Those so often recurring in this book – fear, sadness, anxiety and anger – are the ones most often talked about (see Chapter 7). One bright eight-year-old made a list of things which frightened her: sharks, ghosts, spiders (big), people dying, snakes, rude people (naked), fighting, savage dogs, getting lost, plane crashing, burglars, fire, war, shadows, noises at night, dark, a hand coming out of the wall when she went to the loo at night, bogeymen, dragons. For many children it's a frightening world, far more so than most adults would take seriously, but for the child the fears are very real.

## The Counsellor

### Knowledge
Usually a person who was very important to the child has left the home for whatever reason; how can a child deal with such a major event in the short term and without long-term damage? Much of the

desirable knowledge has been referred to previously in connection with groups. It includes a knowledge of bereavement and possible reactions to it but an acquaintance with bonding and attachment theory should also be added. Child development is crucial because of the different levels of understanding and different reactions at each age. It is also important to have some prior knowledge of how children express their feelings indirectly; for instance, some can show distress by their behaviour or by psychosomatic symptoms, while others react to sadness and loss with depression. Some are reassured by listening to others with similar problems and by sharing their own experiences and feelings with other children.

## Techniques

Counsellors have to be skilled in active listening and in communicating with children both verbally and non-verbally. The kind of counselling described here is short-term and does not involve therapeutic interpretations, though obviously some awareness is required of what a child's remarks might imply in a deeper sense. Thus a four-year-old girl tells the counsellor that her dress is too big – because she feels small inside, or because somebody does not want her to grow up? Or it is a message about nothing being right for her? Another possibility is that someone is treating her like a grown-up. It is one small piece of a puzzle; when others are added to it, what it represents may become clearer.

Counsellors need to avoid crossing the boundary between the professional and the personal. For children to see the counsellor in any other role than that is harmful, especially if they come to see her as an ideal parent, because if that happens the natural parent is undermined. It is important, too, for counsellors to be skilled at ending each session and especially in finishing the final one of the series in a way which leaves the child feeling good about the contact. It is crucial to do this sensitively, so that the ending is not experienced as another loss. Endings can be especially emotive for these children.

When seeing children alone, the most essential skill is the one which is most difficult to describe. It is the ability to empathize with the child's feelings, whatever they are and however inappropriate they may seem to someone else; and it is never safe to presume that the obvious meaning corresponds to what is in the child's mind. Some creative thinking is involved in a gentle rephrasing of what the child says, perhaps using somewhat different words, while noting the assumptions and conveying to the child that the counsellor is trying to understand. An outwardly relaxed manner is necessary but this must hide complete concentration on the child in the room.

A number of children ask if they are the only child I see; the answer is to the effect that at this particular moment no other child matters to me. In fact, the message to the child throughout the session is that he is the only child that I am concerned about now; someone whose views are important, and thus someone who *is* important.

One technique which can be very useful may be called indirect questioning. 'I know you live with Mum but I don't know how often you see Dad' will give a child the message that you are imagining his life, not merely getting a list of facts in the way that 'How often do you see your dad?' might suggest. Repeated comments using different words can expand an issue: 'I'm wondering what that was like for you?'; 'What do you think X meant when he said that?' The technique is nearer to musing than questioning and avoids direct questions where possible. It is one in which praise is irrelevant; its value lies in conveying to the child that he is valued for himself, not simply for what he does.

The ability to stay with children's pain and not change the subject in order to avoid hearing distressing details of the experiences which they have survived is essential, whether seeing children alone or in groups. An eminent judge who sat in on a children's group commented that she found the experience moving and humbling: just what counsellors and group leaders always feel. To be shocked or surprised when they tell their stories is likely to hinder progress; nor are words of sympathy appropriate, though a sympathetic attitude is. While making the child aware of that sympathy in unobtrusive ways the counsellor must follow the details of the child's story closely in order to be alert to the possibility of physical abuse and any indications of sexual abuse. Any signs a child gives of emotional abuse must also be looked for as well as the short- and long-term effects of all of these.


## OTHER HELPING INTERVENTIONS

### Schools

School teachers react in different ways to the behavioural and educational problems of children, many of which are likely to arise from stresses in their family life. More than a few maintain that they are there to teach, not to act as amateur social workers, and that the most important thing they can do for children is to give them the experience of being academically successful; and certainly children who are able to leave home life firmly in the home describe school as a haven. In contrast, other teachers take a broader view, perceiving school as one part of the child's experience. By doing so, and without taking direct action, they can be conscious of the stresses in a child's home life and react with understanding. If there are problems they are aware of the different ways children express them.

Those children who are able successfully to divide their life into compartments so that once they enter the playground they are free to concentrate on doing well, making friends and enjoying learning are usually making good progress. But at the end of the school day the reverse takes place and they return to the anxiety and tensions of home life. Christa was such a child, doing well through a complete separation of the two until her father insisted on coming to her school concert on the same evening as her mother. She was managing a difficult situation by making sure her parents were as separate as possible, and if they had arranged to come on different nights there wouldn't have been a problem. As it was, it was only with great difficulty that her teacher persuaded her to take part in the concert at all.

Even more disturbing for children is to have their feeling of safety shattered by a parent coming into school and trying to take them away by force, an action which affects not only the child involved but other children of separated parents as well and can have wide repercussions.

Sometimes teachers want to help but unwittingly end up doing the opposite because they do what Christa's parents did, they cross a boundary by bringing the stresses of home into school. 'Your dad seems a nice man. Why don't you want to see him, I'm sure he loves you?', asked a young teacher who thought she knew this 'nice' man after talking to him for a few minutes at a parents' consultation meeting. This sort of question may be well-intentioned but is in fact harmful. The child does not want to talk to anyone at school, except perhaps someone she chooses, about something which she finds highly stressful, otherwise she is left feeling that nowhere is safe.

On the other hand, some teachers are very understanding and do a great deal to help an anxious child feel he has an ally. A teacher can be a crucial link in helping him to make a good recovery if that teacher can do what is very difficult; that is, to listen if a child wants to talk about his worries, but not to ask questions and certainly not give advice. Intrusive questions threaten a very delicate balance of relationships in the family and are harmful. Teachers may also help by noting signs of stress in children, especially on Monday mornings, and by reacting with understanding rather than punitively. A child's progress might suffer because of lack of concentration, and this also needs to be handled imaginatively. Some school staff provide more formal counselling, work which should be supervised by a trained person.

A major problem for children at school relates to a loss of confidence in themselves and in particular a loss of ability to make friends. 'Nobody likes me and they won't let me play with them now' is an often voiced comment of these depressed children who, for a while, aren't fun to be with because of their sadness and self-absorption. If your parent has left you, you can't feel too great about yourself. Many are bullied, but too often teachers aren't interested. 'Go and sort it out yourself' was a comment made by a teacher to the seven-year-old who had been knocked on the floor and kicked by three older boys. This is a sad reflection on all schools which condone bullying. 'Miss won't do anything' is a phrase used by many children who are made outcasts by others or who have been taunted by other children because their dad has left.

Too many teachers like to think this sort of thing doesn't happen in their school. The number of children who have made similar remarks about bullying indicates that in all probability, unless the school has taken decisive action and has an anti-bullying policy, it does happen and this confirms the child's belief that adults don't help.

'Miss' could help by making sure these unhappy children are not always the last ones picked for the team, for example, or not made to look small because they are daydreaming. Then there are the ones suffering because their family is poor and can no longer afford the clothes and equipment other children possess. These are children who don't have holidays and haven't been to Woburn Park or Disneyland. In one school in a deprived area one teacher always had a collection of school uniform items and sports gear which she had gathered inconspicuously, as well as other small items poor families have difficulties in buying, such as shoe polish. In many subtle ways an understanding teacher can help children who have lost their peace of mind to gain confidence in themselves.

## A 'GOOD DIVORCE': HOW PARENTS CAN HELP

### What Children Want

Discussion about what children want and need for a good outcome lies at the heart of this book, but it is worth outlining the main points. They are, of course, additional to those which all children want from their parents (see Introduction).

### *To See Dad*

The majority of children want to continue to have a relationship with their dad. They want his support and approval, his love and care; in other words to be special for him. This has to mean more that just seeing him; they want him to be a parent who shows interest and gives encouragement rather than a disciplinarian, one of his roles which is largely not relevant for him any more. It also means they need to know when they will see him next, and for older children especially it is important that he appreciates the need for flexibility and can accept that for healthy development some of their life must be separate from both parents. Where dads live is usually secondary to how they treat their children.

### Mum

As one child said, she wants her old mum back, meaning she wants her mum to be warm and loving and respect her feelings about her dad, however different they might be from her own. Children want their mum to be happy again and look forward with pleasure to what the future may bring.

### Information Shared With Them and Their Opinions Listened To

Children want to be told about things and events that affect them and what changes are likely to take place. They want to be asked for their opinions and to have their views treated with respect, especially when decisions are being made; and they will benefit from knowing that they can ask about anything that worries them without having to protect their parents from possible distress. And for most children the last and most important thing they want to know is that Dad is all right and that he wants to seem them often. To be valued and enjoyed by both parents is a great bonus whether parents live together or apart.

### Parents to be Open and Honest

One of the comments most frequently made by children when they are given the opportunity to talk about their feelings is that nobody listens to them and no one tells them what is happening. If one parent tells the child lies it is bad enough; if both parents do, believing they are protecting their children, they lose all trust in adults. 'Adults tell children lies' is a phrase used by many children whose parents don't live together. One well-meaning mother of a violent husband decided to leave with the children while her husband was out one evening. She told them they had to go shopping but instead went to a refuge. 'If Mum hadn't told me lies I could have taken my teddy with me' said the bereft five-year-old.

Another girl, slightly older, watched her dad packing his things but no one would tell her why or what was happening despite her repeated questions. It is a sad fact that at a time like this parents who are otherwise caring can have so little understanding of what a child might feel in such circumstances. The next day her mum told her that her dad had gone for good; she said that she and her mum cried a lot but now things are better because there are fewer rows and Mum and Dad are happier. She had been worried she would not see him again and felt very lonely for a time, but in fact it is all right now as she does see him. She thought it was his fault because he wouldn't come home from the pub until late but, despite this, she loves him best and for a long time wished she lived with him. Now she accepts that this would not have been possible and thinks the present arrangements are the best there could be. She is no longer worried and is beginning to enjoy life again. A bad start can be put right.

There is also the question, what should children *not* be told? Obviously, it is not appropriate to discuss with them details of adult relationships and neither should they share financial anxieties. It is only matters which concern them that they should know about and most of all they want to be reassured that both parents are managing well.

*Parental Hostility*

Children are used by parents in many different ways, including being treated as an adult or told secrets. They have enough problems in growing up successfully without being overwhelmed with inappropriate emotional loads.

There is some evidence that children involved in parental battles may not do as well as they could at school. Their anxieties affect their concentration, as does the lack of self-worth which results from living in a hostile atmosphere. Anger, anxiety and being exposed to adults who relate to each other without any warmth undermines them. One eleven-year-old brought up in what might have been a highly damaging atmosphere did nevertheless manage well because of a close tie with his maternal grandmother who gave him the care and concern which was not forthcoming in his own home.

At the time of separation, all children, without exception, want any hostility to stop. Whether hostility between parents is more damaging to the child than the separation itself has been the subject of debate. One view is that unless the conflict is expressed violently, is not finally resolved or is such that the child feels caught in the middle, 'there does not appear to be a direct relationship between parents' conflict *per se* and a child's subsequent well-being' (Rodgers and Pryor 1998, p. 41). The implication is that family relationships rather than the break-up do the greater harm. However, these findings should be viewed with caution (Hooper 1994, p. 89), because there are too many situations in which children react differently, even within the same family, to give an accurate picture.

Two teenage boys were talking about how it was before their parents separated. The older one said it was fairly peaceful, there were a few rows but not anything terrible; the younger one said for some months it was absolutely awful, they shouted and screamed at each other and a number of times he remembered one or the other leaving the house when they were arguing. Two very different views of the same event, both expressing their own 'truth'.

It is particularly unfortunate that hostility is most likely to be expressed at the beginning and end of contact visits, when, almost inevitably, it is witnessed by the child and thus negates much of the good the contact visit might have done. As a general rule, the sooner the matrimonial conflict ends, the less likely the children are to be harmed in the future.

For many children caught up in a war which is not of their making it is members of their family whom they find most helpful. Often grandparents, especially grandmothers, are the most trusted: 'I tell my secrets to my Gran' is a frequent comment. Less numerous are those who find sympathetic listeners in aunts and uncles or older siblings, though one nine-year-old always felt supported on contact visits by her four-year-old brother but 'of course he didn't understand'. These family members are a very important part of the child's ability to survive well. Grandparents especially have usually been around for the whole of a child's life. They are less emotionally involved than mums and dads and are in a better position to be the source of information about the family history when the child is ready to know. Those who give continuity and loving care play a crucial part in many a child's good outcome.

Much more needs to be known about why some children are harmed in this way and others little or not at all. For those in the second category, or some of them, the explanation may be that from their very early years they have never known anything else but violence in the home and this can continue even after the separation, almost as a way of life. Other couples lived in relative peace until the event, often infidelity, occurred that led to the divorce. Then the hostility can be of shorter duration but very intense at the time of separation. After they have separated, parents like these may manage to contain their angry feelings when their children are around and don't forget that if they are upstairs in bed they may still be able to hear the angry exchanges.

These are some of the very varied patterns and responses to hostility within the family. How severely children are harmed by it is modified in so many different ways by tensions in the home and the quality of parenting they receive from each parent. So how should the debate about hostility proceed? Whether the reordering of families through changes of partner is of greater significance than hostility is not likely to be a helpful question because they may be linked. Other factors, cumulative in their effect, such as poverty, the quality of life of the family, and the personality and mental health of the parents, are not subjected to the same scrutiny. Good experiences also have to be brought into the equation.

The term 'harm' to children also needs to be clarified. On general grounds the expectation is that harm, besides being physical, may also be psychological, causing the children to be timid, aggressive or anxious to the extent that it interferes with their functioning in different areas of their life. But, to repeat one of the basic tenets of this book, positive experiences can counter the negative so that not a few children whose confidence was destroyed by experiences of the kind described above do recover. Some regain their confidence completely; others who have not been so fortunate are left with a view of themselves which, although not crippling, is nevertheless a part of their personality for many years, or even a lifetime.

*Parent Distress is Likely to be Temporary*
It can be helpful for children to be told that the parent they live with might be distressed by the ending of the relationship and will not be as patient and loving as they would like, and that sometimes the parent him- or herself might need some understanding. These parents may deal with their distress by being angry; if this is the situation children might benefit from knowing that the anger is not because they have done anything wrong; in fact, it is probably nothing to do with them.

## Signs That Intervention Has Helped

How do we know the child has been helped to a good recovery? Some of the signs will be short-term; others long-term. For the former we might listen to what a child says. The words: 'It was like lots of doors opening in my head', indicated that some of the worries had been shared or perceived differently. A new confidence is another obvious sign, and with it a growing ability to deal with situations in a positive way. One effect of this new approach will be reflected in progress at school, more friends and resuming enjoyment of activities after they had been lost for a time. Life becomes child-centred again. The opportunity to talk could also help the child to accept the situation between parents, even if it is not what the child wants. Another short-term sign, one shared by all children who have been through a traumatic time, is a physical growth spurt, perhaps an indication that energy used in worrying is redirected into growing and developing.

In the long term these children are less likely to be among those who talk of separating parents as being a life sentence. Quite often a residue of sadness does remain but at least this will not dominate the child's life. Despite the fact that much research suggests that children are more likely to have difficulties socially and educationally, and also experience poor health, unemployment and other disadvantages as adults, the children will have some positive experiences. Sharing their thoughts and feelings at a time of crisis can be one of these good experiences and is important because it could increase confidence which in turn brings its own gains.

Parents' own confidence must not be forgotten. Donald Winnicott, an eminent psychoanalyst, wrote about 'good-enough mothering' (Winnicott 1971, p. 10); 'good-enough parenting' is more appropriate today. A perfect parent, if there were such a thing, would not be good for children.

For children, if both their parents play a part in making it a 'good divorce' for them, there is a very good chance that they will grow up little harmed as adults.

# 10   Parents Who Live Apart

About one in twenty families are headed by lone parents, of whom all but about one in seven are women. Many are poor. Most are concerned for their children and, despite having few resources, do their best in very difficult circumstances.

Lone parents are likely to have strong, conflicting feelings about their separation; sadness and disappointment that the relationship has failed, even despair, are general but also anxiety that they might be doing harm to their children. Even the parent who instigated the separation could, and often does, have such feelings; divorce is difficult for almost everyone. There is no ritual to mark the end of the marriage and the reactions of relatives and friends will vary: 'You did the right thing, you would never be happy with her'; 'It's not your fault; she can't expect you to be faithful all your life'; or, 'It's right to leave him, whatever he promises he will never stop drinking'; 'You should stay together because of the children.'

## Family Patterns

There are many different family patterns. As many as one-third of lone mothers have never lived with the father of their child; some of their problems, especially poverty, are shared with those with broken relationships, but their feelings about being a single mother can be quite different from, and as varied as, the feelings of those who have separated from a partner. They are increasing in number and quite often are young mothers. Some of them regret being alone; others welcome it in the expectation that they and their children will be happier. Some are in caring lesbian relationships and a number live with their own mother, the children often 'granny-reared'. Children in this situation sometimes derive great benefit from the care and concern of an extended family.

Little is known about the effect on children of never having had the experience of knowing a father, yet if poverty and hostility are not present and a caring relationship is, it appears quite likely that they will do well. However, according to one study, children born to and living with single women tended, on average, to do better than those who subsequently lived with both parents or a step-parent. Of the latter group, those who do badly have experienced conflict, violence or cold and critical parents (Burghes 1994).

Only in a small proportion of separations are women the ones who leave the family. Society is less tolerant of this than of fathers leaving, unless there has been domestic violence or abuse. This can be more difficult for the children as the mothers have usually been the primary carer and it is broadly true that they are more aware of feelings and able to listen to their children, though this is changing. ChildLine found that of those who rang them, a far higher proportion of children living with lone fathers had problems causing them actively to seek help. They were quite largely concerned with the inability of their dads to share caring feelings (Childline 1998, p. 32).

Children brought up by one biological parent and one step-parent form another large group which can consist of these three, or both partners may bring children from a previous relationship into the new one. If these new units also fail further complicated patterns follow. The children in such a case pay a price; quite often, once the initial difficulties have been sorted out and the new family has settled down, close ties are formed, only to be dissolved when the unit breaks up. It is no wonder that they may be amongst the most emotionally harmed (Cockett and Tripp 1994, p. 35). Having twice lost security in their lives, the message they take from their experience, rightly or wrongly, is that adults can never be trusted. Once again they are left feeling hurt because they became fond of somebody else who went away.

It is precisely the very wide variety in the patterns of family life that make many of the popular generalizations of little use. For instance, if there are such things as 'family values' they are very hard to define given the complexity of late twentieth-century family patterns, but if the phrase connotes loving care and concern for a child, the two-parent family certainly does not have a monopoly. 'Family Values' is in fact the title of a Home Office consultation paper (November 1998) which suggested more generous subsidies to poor working families, much needed extra money for childcare, sixteen-year-olds in education and programmes such as Homestart, a volunatary scheme which offers support and practical help to families with young children. These are important, helpful proposals, but another idea of granting automatic rights for single fathers needs more careful thought unless there is some provision to explore what the quality of parenting was like when the family was intact.

The 'quality of parenting', to use a current popular phrase, is increasingly thought of as more important than the structure of the family. It refers to the warmth of the relationship between parent and child and the concern parents have to meet the child's emotional needs; mutual pleasure between child and parent is also an important element. All these forward the growth and development of the child.

## Negative Influences

It is arguable that one of the key issues of a successful marriage, and also of a satisfactory separation, is managing the almost inevitable conflict between couples; and the reason why this is so important is because of the potential negative effect it has on children. Children are sometimes directly involved in conflict – an aggressive husband is likely to be aggressive towards the children. In other families children witness the aggression but, although they might live in fear of being hurt, are not actively involved. For many, it is a familiar pattern as their parents, whether one or both, have always been aggressive to each other; in other words, parental conflict existed long before the separation (Cherlin et al. 1991).

Continuing parental conflict after separation is associated with the risk of a poor outcome for the children (Kelly 1993), though this is only one of the potential negative factors. Which of them is the most damaging is a matter for debate. Research in Exeter led to the conclusion that conflict was associated with a poor outcome but raised the question of whether the effect was as bad as is thought (Cockett and Tripp 1994). Other research emphasized the quality of contact as a significant factor and also the effect of multiple changes (Rodgers and Pryor 1998). Another possible negative factor is the loss of parent by separation which, it has been claimed, carries the risk that children will repeat the parental pattern of breakdown (Cockett and Tripp 1994, p. 60). Which of all these factors, to which must be added poverty and social conditions, is the most significant will vary according to the circumstances of each child.

*Poverty*
The social setting of the family has to be taken into account. A higher proportion of British families live in poverty than in any country in the European Union except Ireland (*UN Human Development Report* 1998). Very many of these families are headed by lone parents. Perhaps the major implication of this for the present work is that members of such families experience a high level of anxiety which is a direct result of the difficulties in surviving with inadequate resources.

Such lone parents can feel that they are failures. This is an understandable reaction to not being part of the main stream of society; instead, their situation can make people feel undervalued and inadequate. In these circumstances, unless there is a supporting network, it is difficult for parents to give children time for child-centred activities and stimulation. Ongoing parental rows or being cared for by a parent who is depressed or not managing well, especially around the time of separation, can jeopardize the children's stability, security and sometimes safety.

Poverty adds greatly to the stresses in a family headed by a single parent. It can produce a whole cycle of problems, affecting the quality of mothering and resulting in her being less available to help her child with school work and provide stimuli to widen the child's horizons. In addition she is depressed because she cannot afford the books or school outings and extras which would help. In consequence the child tends to fall behind academically, may fail to get the qualifications needed for further training, and in the end may take unskilled work. It is the continuing disadvantages which are damaging, not the number of parents bringing up children. Children who experience poverty and discordant, quarrelsome families are likely to go on experiencing similar environments as they grow up (Rutter and Rutter 1992, p. 33–4).

Throughout, the confidence of the lone parent is undermined, her physical and mental health is affected and not infrequently she attempts to solve her problems by actions which might put her at risk in some way. If she becomes pregnant her problems can be compounded. But this pattern is not inevitable and the cycle can be broken by extra income providing there is support for the family, including that of statutory bodies, voluntary organizations or groups such as Ginger-bread and school staff; these can all provide some good experiences to counter the negative ones. Good experiences too, are cumulative.

Poverty is arguably the most urgent issue for lone parents (Mac-Dermott et al. 1998). The General Household Survey showed that in 1996 a third of lone mothers with dependent children had an income of under £100 a week at a time when 48 per cent of married parents had a weekly income exceeding £500, though the average number of children of lone mothers was slightly smaller, 1.7 compared with 1.9. The lone mothers without other resources who cannot work will be markedly worse off, though for those able to work, a working families tax credit is proposed for the future. These provisions will not be adequate for this social group of society; the United Kingdom has the lowest level of publicly funded childcare provision for the under-threes in the European Union (Child Poverty Action Group 1998).

As a result of their situation, many of the nation's children are in poor health and suffer from both physical and emotional problems, and what is even more worrying is the finding that children under five years at the time of the parents' divorce are particularly vulnerable (Dominian et al. 1991).

## Mothers With Custody

The feelings of mothers at the time of separation are varied, complex and confusing. Some are pleased the relationship has ended; for example, in situations where neither partner has any warm feelings for the other and both are pleased to be freed from the tensions and antagonism of a loveless relationship. Their concern in these circumstances can be for the children.

But for others, denial is often the first reaction – 'This can't be happening, he'll be back'; 'We've had worse rows than this and it's been all right'; 'He's weak, it's that woman's fault, I would like to strangle her'; 'He deceived me and broke promises to the children and rubbished a relationship that maybe wasn't marvellous but wasn't any worse than other people's.' The abandoned wife at times will want revenge and to hurt her ex-partner as she has been hurt, but at other times she feels nothing, or simply feels numb and depressed. These changing moods make her wonder if she is going mad. There may be physical symptoms of tension, or self-blame, but then a return to her thinking it wasn't her fault: he told lies; he drank too much. He is selfish.

Not only are there many different patterns to be considered, there is also the complexity of every aspect of separating parents and the many different effects on their children. Mothers alone are no exception; their reactions are not only varied but go through radical changes with time, though it would be true to say that for the majority the concern for their children is paramount. Once they have accepted that this time the separation is final the initial reaction for many is of despair at what they perceive to be the monumental task in front of them. But in time, which may be one year, two years, or more, the strength of these feelings diminishes as the pattern of the future becomes clearer and acceptance takes its place. The last feeling at the end of this long emotional journey is one of growing confidence and hope for the new life ahead.

There are lone mothers, though, who see the situation differently. They may feel that however bad an experience it was, they still love their ex-partner and cherish the hope of a reconciliation, while others say they love him but can't live with him because trust has gone. His behaviour wasunacceptable in many ways, but nevertheless they still remain emotionally tied. These couples who no longer love each other but are still concerned are among those who manage 'a good divorce' for their children.

Those who, after the devastating experience of being rejected, recover with some help and a lot of determination, say that, in truth, the divorce was the best thing that happened for them personally. Charles, a rather dapper man in a suit, left his wife Sheila for his secretary, a much younger woman skilled in socializing. Sheila had been easy-going and homely and, without resentment, had been dominated by her husband. He expected to continue this relationship after the divorce but once she was on her own she found a hitherto unknown strength and, against all odds, demanded her rights. In doing so her children were freed from having to worry about her, and she became a different person, one who was much happier in her new, confident role, though it took Charles some time to realize he could no longer intimidate her.

Most lone mothers will have had some prior idea of the stresses to come although they are hardly likely to have appreciated the strength of the feeling of loneliness or the crippling lack of confidence. For some it is the intensity of their anger which was unexpected. An anxiety about whether they were going out of their minds because of the fearful bizarre images and obsessive thoughts in their mind is also not uncommon.

One teenager said she had lost both parents: her father because he had moved to a different town and she did not see him often, and her mother because she had changed such a lot. She screamed and shouted over very small things, hit all the children without any obvious cause and posed a frightening threat for them all by constantly threatening suicide. 'I know she can't cope with Dad leaving', said the teenager, 'but I have my feelings too and I can't cope with Mum for much longer. There is absolutely nothing we children can do which is OK.' Her solution was to give up her plan to stay on at school and to leave home after taking her exams. Her mother's despair, expressed in a way her daughter described as 'behaving like a crazy woman' is difficult for the child to understand and deal with, despite her wish to help her.

### Responsibilities and Feelings

For the lone mother to have sole responsibility for the family, having usually to manage with less money and at the same time being anxious about the forthcoming changes, is not something to relish.

The changes might include having to relinquish the family home, find a job, pay for childcare and deal with many things for the first time, such as bills and taxes, and carrying out practical jobs of repair and maintenance of car, garden or house.

It is understandable and helpful if, for a short time, she can rely on emotional support from an older son or daughter using him or her as a confidant, but this is not a situation which should continue for any length of time. This is because if the attachment is too close for too long and the mother comes to depend exclusively on the child, the daughter can feel guilt at having or wanting her own life. She perceives herself as half of a pair, never one complete person, always guilty because Mum is lonely and at home by herself. Children in this situation can be voluntary prisoners, their sleep broken by nightmares, their idle moments disturbed by painful flashes of memory. As one child said, 'Sometimes you have to love them like another grown-up would, because they can get depressed.' At the time of separation younger children want extra comfort but, for example, to share the mother's bed for a long time will not be in their own interests either.

In addition, the mother will have to deal with the emotional needs of her children who are likely to have a very different perception of Dad, and what happened and why, from her own. Keith, a teenager, was angry with his dad on his own behalf, and more significantly on his mother's, because his dad had left his mother for a girlfriend, leaving Keith feeling that he did not want to have anything to do with his father. Although this is probably not the best emotional outcome in the long term, it can be regarded as the easiest alternative because it avoided a conflict of loyalties and ensured that Keith had a secure place by Mum's side. When, in time, he understands that she is coping very well and doesn't need his support any more, he may feel freer to made up his own mind about the reasons for the divorce and be able to restore the loving relationship with his dad which he had allowed to be dominated by his anger.

A mother may have to contain her negative feelings about her ex-husband in front of the children and at the same time feel she must protect them from the pain of broken promises by making excuses which she knows are not true; for example, making up for forgotten birthdays by sending cards 'with love from Daddy'. In a situation where the absent father has rejected the children, whether temporarily or not, it might be better for children to know that at least one parent won't deceive them, however painful the truth and however well-intentioned the deception might be. The tasks are to help the children, very gently, to appreciate the reality that Dad is very involved with his new life at the moment and to ensure that, whatever happens, they will not be told any lies and any changes which affect them will be discussed with them. This will not be a happy period for the whole family and takes time before changes take place.

It is not easy for the mother to deal which such emotive situations at a time when she is likely to have less emotional energy to sort out the problems and worries than she would like. This, though, is a temporary phase and with time the situation improves. It is very different from that of people with long-term personality problems. Paranoid personalities, who distrust any warm overtures and experience every attempt at closeness as an attack, create problems if the children, in their concern for their parent, become closely involved with them.

Eleven-year-old George lived with his vocal and flamboyant mother who, despite the post-divorce antagonism between her and her ex-husband, believed her son had no problems. In reality he was deeply troubled because he loved his dad very much but was unable to express his feelings because of his mother's vehemently expressed hate for his father. Rather than risk losing his mother too, he believed that he had no alternative but to appear as a bright, happy, problem-free child. He attempted to deal with his feelings of anger by spending hour after hour in front of his computer playing games of violence.

Some lone mothers avoid poverty by working full-time. They will have to juggle with their commitments in order to reconcile the conflicting interests of work, childcare and running a home. After an eight-hour working day a tired parent who needs to unwind but instead has to feed her family and deal with a multitude of household matters, is not able to meet the demands of children as well as she would like. They might be feeling marginalized or, worse, feel rejected and desperate for parental time and love. Of course, some children receive excellent childcare from caring parent substitutes, but if this is not the situation they can be emotionally deprived even though the mother is doing her very best for them. This is an example of the consequences of divorce being more damaging than the separation itself. It is a situation which also occurs in two-parent families, where both parents work long hours.

### Fathers With Custody

Some of the problems of the fathers bringing up their children are the same as those of lone mothers, although for many lone fathers the one most difficult to resolve is that of employment and childcare. Some are able to make satisfactory arrangements with relatives, friends or child-minders and it is likely that afterschool activity centres will be more available in the future.

Some choose to give up employment to care for the children themselves, a solution which leads to another problem, that of finding a satisfactory social life for themselves. It is one in which befriending schemes might play an important part. They can feel, or be made to feel by some mothers, that they are usurping women's traditional role and in consequence are treated with hostility at times. They, like mothers, can be affected by poverty but one of the gains is that boys will be brought up by a parent of the same sex as themselves which can be beneficial, especially for older ones, providing the father is a good model for them to emulate. Older boys are often more concerned about living in a male environment; girls in any event are more likely to live with their mother.

But lone fathers can have emotional problems too. Some are caring for the children because their mother, for a variety of reasons, is not considered by the court to be the more suitable parent. Others had wives who, by choice, left not only them but their children too. In these circumstances it can be difficult to contain the hurt and anger; feelings which, unless actually faced, can have a long-term destructive influence on the children's development and on the father's future relationships. He may try to stop the children having contact with their mother; he regards their desire to do so as a rejection of him rather than something normal and understandable.

Those with custody can sometimes find dealing with their teenage daughter brings problems because, no longer a child, she can be a constant reminder of a wife who rejected him. The need of a child to be independent may be especially difficult for a lone parent. The punishment a lone father is likely to give a defiant girl is to ground her, forbidding her to go out so that she can't meet her friends and develop relationships – with boys.

Other children have to deal with being rejected by their mother, especially if she has left for a new partner. If Mum doesn't want you or love you then you can expect nothing, your self-esteem is zero. To recover well, a lot of loving from Dad and friends and relatives and perhaps skilled help, too, might be needed. This role puts an extra responsibility on the lone father who quite often finds it difficult, if not impossible, to meet these demands. Many caring fathers have had to learn to give their children time and to demonstrate affection in a more open way.

In the majority of homes fathers never expected to be involved with the day-to-day care of their children. When they were married they enjoyed the 'quality time' spent with them and were supportive and helpful about all their activities but they also found their work satisfying as well as essential to support the family. However, when good part-time dads have to became full-time carers the situation changes completely. Quite often, for financial, practical or emotional reasons, there is no alternative to his continuing his job. Given these pressures his work may sometimes be used as an excuse for doing little in the home and expecting the children to clean the house, cook the meals and bring up younger siblings.

A father who in these circumstances fails to consider the children's feelings about the tasks he imposes on them or to value what they do is not contributing towards their well-being. Obviously, it is right that children help in an age-appropriate way towards the running of the home, but it is not in their interests if they have excessive responsibility or cannot enjoy leisure activities or their childhood. In some areas there are voluntary organizations which can help with problems of this kind and enable such families to enjoy a proper social life.

## Non-Resident Fathers

Fathers leave the marital home for many different reasons which converge and conflict. For many it is the need to feel good about themselves; perhaps they have felt criticized and devalued. Life, they felt, was passing them by and there was no pleasure in anything; they wanted to feel special to somebody. These may be difficult feelings to discuss for those who are unused to expressing feelings in words; they are more at home talking about practical matters than their emotions. Some feel they tried to make changes but did not succeed. There was no way they could bring any happiness into the family: get out before it is too late. There might be guilt because of the children's distress, and anger because his ex-wife has got the house and kids and now she wants all the money she can get. 'If she cared about the children she would make it as easy as possible for me to see them', he thinks; 'It's difficult anyway because I don't know what to say to them. She's selfish.'

The non-resident father is just as likely not to be free from anxiety and often has very painful feelings about his failed marriage. If he instigated the divorce, he might regret very deeply the diminished contact with his children and the risk of his influence on them declining, especially if he lives some distance away from them. His emotions may cause psychosomatic symptoms or depression; or he may drink too much or become physically ill.

One way of trying to continue the relationship, though not the

marriage, may be by insisting on contact with the children in the belief
that any connection, however hostile, is better than none. One sad
and striking example was the father who had very little contact with
his two children when the family were together but after he left and
married for a second time he used his ex-wife as a scapegoat for his
deep feelings of inadequacy; he and his new partner united in making
her life as difficult as possible, using the children in furtherance of this
damaging task.

In contrast, a father can maintain that despite all that has
happened he still loves his ex-partner. This loving might be for the
person he married who changed over time and became more mature
and responsible. It is much less likely that he loves the self-confident
person she has become since the separation. Now she has become a
stronger person who has coped with many changes and new situations, he has been left behind. Unless the couple, before either embark
on a new relationship, have some idea about what part they played in
the break-up and its roots in their childhood, there is a risk that the
problems will be repeated and affect a new relationship.

In one family a father whose marriage had ended by mutual
agreement missed his children greatly; he saw them as often as he
could manage, despite the physical distance between them. He said it
was like being outside, in the dark, silently looking into a well-lit room
where his family were. This must be a feeling experienced by many
fathers who would not be able to explain their loss so vividly.

There are many factors to be overcome by fathers who miss their
children and desperately want to see them. Hostility between parents
has been mentioned a number of times but remarriage of either
partner also needs delicate negotiation because of the feelings of all
those involved. The co-operation of the resident parent can also be
crucial, especially if young children are involved.

A proportion of fathers join pressure groups, such as Families Need
Fathers, in England, or Fathers demand Rights, in Canada. In one
project thirty-two members were interviewed in Ontario (Bertoia and
Drakich 1995), most of whom said that they believed that the law
discriminated against them in giving the mothers custody. Yet on
closer examination it appeared that most had not applied for custody
and did not want it. They were not interested in the day-to-day care of
their children but in what is called 'quality time', meaning the
freedom to choose when they saw their children for leisure activities.

Non-resident fathers often wanted to be involved in the decision
making over matters which concerned their children. It is probable
that their concern was more about power and control than equal rights
or their children's well-being. They also thought they were having to

pay far too much for childcare though in reality, as in England after divorce, it is the ex-husbands who are better off, and the resident wives who are poorer. This small Canadian research project confirms the opinion based on my own experience, that it is the reduction in the power and control they have over their families which is irksome for many fathers.

For fathers, anger after separation can be related to their ex-partner having a new boyfriend or partner; this is a frequent sticking point and is not modified by their having a new wife or girlfriend themselves. For these fathers such a situation is experienced as a rejection and gives rise to an unacknowledged jealousy, which can be dealt with by vengeful acts. These often involve the children and contact visits can thus be fraught with difficulties. Carol's father had managed contact visits very well until his ex-wife found a new partner and became pregnant, after which he made life as difficult as he could for her. He refused all reasonable requests for flexibility regarding Carol's meeting with him, and constantly denigrated the mother to Carol – 'Your mum's a slag, a bad mother, she doesn't care for you', and so on. He aggravated the problems by not paying maintenance on time. This previously reasonable man appeared to have lost the ability to be co-operative and was oblivious to the harm he was doing to his daughter. Another repeated pattern designed to aggravate the ex-partner is to return the children home late – or early – from contact visits.

Five-year-old Peter's parents had not been married and had never lived together. His mother, despite subsequently marrying and having a stable relationship with someone else, felt she had to agree to the father's having parental rights because of pressure from her solicitor. During contact meetings Peter had to listen to his father making disparaging remarks about his mother and showed his distress by wetting his bed on the following three or four nights after every visit, though he would never say what was worrying him. It appeared that he was aware he was being used to upset his mother by a man deeply resentful of the new-found happiness she had with her husband.

## Step-Parents

'Step-parent' is used rather loosely here as many so-called step-parents are not married. It refers to the new partner of a biological parent, whether they are married or not. Stepmothers and stepfathers have roles that differ from each other in a number of respects. What follows is a brief discussion of certain aspects of step-family relationships;

many excellent books deal with the topic more fully (for example, Gorill, Barnes, Thompson and Buchardt (eds) 1998).

As a generalization, to be a stepmother is the more difficult. The importance of her gradual entry into the family and an awareness of what her arrival on the scene is like for children is not always appreciated. She is usually the one who makes the rules and is concerned with running the house, despite often working full-time. She is more likely than the stepfather to set limits, to decide how things will be done and generally to make sure the new family is functioning well. Older children can resent these new arrangements and girls in particular may have feelings of rivalry with this woman who is running their lives. It is a difficult task for children and adults alike.

A stepmother's relationship with her newly acquired family will be conducted in a different way from their natural mother's, especially in the areas which she does not approve of: 'Our Mum lets us choose our cereal'; 'We always had our supper sitting in front of the telly.' She might have to deal with attempts to test her, or her valiant efforts to be a good mum are rejected: 'No thank you; we don't do it that way.' But as earlier chapters showed, many do succeed, to everyone's benefit.

Stepfathers normally have less to do with the children and tend to be less skilful in understanding their feelings, though of course there are many exceptions. They, too, may be given a tough time by the children, but it is not likely to be quite so stressful. This is because most fathers are usually less involved with the emotional side of caring, and are commonly happier showing they care by doing rather than showing their feelings; they mend bikes, know about computers and can talk about football, often making it easier for children to accept a stepfather than a stepmother. As long as they provide a loving base for the family, are seen by the children as both strong and supportive and do not attempt to be a disciplinarian or 'Dad' until the children are ready, the chances of a successful relationship with their stepchildren are high.

To the children's problem of adjusting to a new step-parent may be added the additional complications and stress of uniting children and stepchildren in the same family. This often can take place without a time lapse for them to adjust to the changes in their lives and having less money and smaller accommodation, because of the expenses incurred in supporting a previous family. Understanding and a determination to make it work are the essentials for success. Accommodation can be a flashpoint: to share a bedroom with other children who are strangers, to be an only girl with two or three stepbrothers or to have to deal with rivalry. One says, 'He's my dad'; the other comes back with, 'No he isn't now, he's my dad.' These are the sort of situations to which solutions have to be found, preferably before they happen, or certainly as soon as possible afterwards. Where parents can foresee impending areas of conflict, children, after some initial difficulty in accepting the changes, are likely to settle well, providing they think it is 'fair'.

For biological mothers it is the thought of another woman caring for her children which is hard to accept and may lead to attempts to increase the difficulties between her and her own ex-partner. Mothers sometimes do not like the idea of a woman who is a stranger bathing their own small children, putting them to bed and carrying out other intimate acts. They can feel usurped and angry and always have the fear that the children will prefer this new person to their 'real' mum. Such a fear of rejection is hard to bear. In addition, the child's mother can often be very anxious about the child's safety, especially if she has experienced an abusive relationship with her ex-partner.

Despite all these possible pitfalls, those concerned bring to their changed situation a will to find happiness and their own strengths and survival techniques.

# 11   CONTACT

## Some of the Difficulties

Contact visits put father and child in an artificial situation, and this is especially so if the father does not have his own home. Some children feel disloyal to their mother if they show too much enjoyment of the visits; a reaction Dad can easily misinterpret, particularly if he finds it difficult to relate to a child he may not have known well, or if he does not feel confident in this situation. In addition, he is attempting to entertain a growing child whom he sees intermittently, and who has rapidly changing interests. Some enjoy the idea of parenthood and believe they love their child but the actual close relationships with the necessary time and patience needed for good parenting are neither welcomed nor enjoyed.

The activities which take place during the visits should, of course, be age-appropriate, but it is better if there is a routine that could include a non-emotive shared activity such as drawing, which gives the child the opportunity to talk and is symbolically important; it is good for the child to have a corner of his own in Dad's house so that he feels he belongs there too. The rituals need to change as the child grows; a small child, for instance, will want to start with a hug, whereas a drink and biscuit with dad might be more appropriate for an older child. Despite its being written a number of years ago, Rowlands' *Saturday Parent* (1980) is still particularly relevant and is a very useful and helpful book with many important insights and ideas to make the visits more enjoyable for both.

Careful preparation is important, as Rowlands stresses, if the visit is to be a success, with contingency plans in case things go wrong with the arrangements, and attention to details such as making sure the child has all the necessary clothes or equipment which will be needed. And there must be discussion between the former partners about the different rules in different houses: the timing and rituals of bedtimes, for instance; how and when homework is done; how often the child should phone the other parent and many other details.

Where co-operation does not exist, every contact visit can reinforce a child's concern about conflict. For example, at the beginning of the visit a non-resident parent may make the child remove all his clothes and put on those which belong in his house, changing again at the end of the visit. Other fathers refuse to let the child take any toy out of the house, even 'just to show Mummy'. It is difficult to see what message they expect the child to receive from such actions and how either can help the child. Parents have ceased to be partners but this does not give them the right to be uncooperative with their ex-partner to the detriment of the child. Mothers, too, can and sometimes do, behave in ways which are harmful, whether by verbal hostility to Dad or by refusing to acknowledge the child's pleasure at a special outing, for example.

It is virtually certain that children will not see the separation in quite the same way as the parent. Most will try very hard not to take sides, but others believe that Dad, who, in their mother's eyes, might be uncaring and irresponsible, is the very best person in the world. And even if mothers know they should be pleased that the children are seeing him, it is not always possible to be enthusiastic about the expensive toy he has bought or the horse-riding lessons he pays for, when he won't pay child benefit regularly or find money for a school trip.

Some non-resident parents are caring but lack empathy and have no idea of the impact of what they say on their child. 'Your new family' is a phrase some children find upsetting because of the implication that the family they have always known is 'old' and in some way second-best. One small four-year-old soiled herself and amidst her tears told her mother that Daddy said he would get her a new Mummy and she didn't want another one, she was very happy with the one she had.

A separated father will experience other practical and emotional difficulties, probably including having more expenses and having to find suitable accommodation. Arranging contact with his children and reconciling these meetings with having to earn a living, especially if he does not have a suitable place for the children to visit, or the children live a long way away, can cause a great deal of stress. Perhaps it is not surprising that a third of fathers lose contact straight away and after five years only half see their children frequently.

There are many reasons for this. A recurring one is that the repeated partings are found to be too painful for some fathers, and this can be a perfectly genuine reason, though they are more likely to say that the partings upset the children rather than themselves and therefore contact visits are not worth continuing. This excuse is far from the whole truth; guilt can inhibit them as parents. It is as if the father has to punish himself by believing that his children have rejected him, therefore he opts out of maintaining contact with them.

Contact can be broken in a very different way by fathers who equate paying child support with a right to see their child; if the mother is reluctant for the visits to take place or refuses outright and the father retaliates by not maintaining them (despite the law), it will be the children who are affected the most as they will not see their father.

Sometimes a father's difficulties relate to the feelings of his new partner who finds the children a threat or sees them as rivals for their dad's affection, a feeling which can be reciprocated by the children. 'He always kisses her and talks to her first when he comes home. I hate her', said a twelve-year-old, who, like many children in that situation, complained that she never saw her dad alone. One very distraught father had been told by his new partner that he had to choose between her and his six-year-old son whom he loved deeply. He chose her; one could only guess what the long-term effect would be on this little boy who, soon afterwards, could be described as suffering from depression; he became lethargic, stopped eating and no longer played with his friends.

Where differences with the ex-partner have not been resolved for the non-resident parent, life is not without its problems. It may be difficult for people so placed to accept that they cannot see their children when they want to but have to follow a routine; something they cannot control and which they have to accept with reluctance. Others desperately want to see their children, although returning to the family home to confront hostility and pain, whether expressed openly or not, is an effort; one father described it as 'running the gauntlet'. Collecting and returning the child from contact visits can become an emotional hurdle, a high price to pay for maintaining contact with children, but one which, fortunately, many of them feel worthwhile.

This, of course, is only the beginning; where do you take them on a wet February weekend when you are short of money and the growing children seem almost like strangers? An age gap between them also makes for problems because they want to do different things, whether going to the park, going swimming, watching a favourite programme on the television or going to a football match. It can be disheartening if a father has arranged a special treat and is then told, 'That's boring.' Angry children are not without skill when it comes to making a difficult situation worse.

The children of those fathers who spent little time in the marital home when the family was intact may well have a picture of Dad which has been filtered through their mother. Daddy will be pleased you did well at school, have been picked for the team or whatever, but he has not been around to be told face to face. Consequently, contact would be infrequent and he would have very little experience of involvement with his children. For these fathers to engage in child-centred activities with pleasure can be difficult; they may not know what is age-appropriate and it is easy to forget the child is growing and developing and how much fashions in clothes or toys matter. Knowledge about how long children of different ages can concentrate and the sorts of things which amuse them, the books they enjoy and the things they can do to encourage their independence is all-important. 'I wish Daddy wouldn't put my coat on for me', says five-year-old Karen, 'I've been doing it since I was four.' 'I keep telling Dad I wash my hair myself,' says Mark, 'but he won't listen to me.'

If these fathers are to take their responsibilities as lone parents seriously, they need information and knowledge about children at different ages and about their needs. They can, almost in desperation, give treats which, because of their frequency, become essential for the child: 'What toy are you going to buy me this week?' But this is not what the child really wants, though the treats and presents can succeed in antagonizing the struggling mother even further, if she lets it.

Sharing the pleasure of buying a present together might be a better option than buying an elaborate model aeroplane for a five-year-old son. Unfortunately, sharing with a child and finding mutual pleasure in doing things together is something alien to many fathers – still, it is never too late to learn and the benefits are enormous providing the child is seen as he is and not as a make-believe child. Debbie's father refused to show any interest in his daughter's progress in football; his daughter should be cute and feminine and anyway girls don't play football. He wanted a fantasy daughter, not the flesh and blood one who only wanted her dad to love her as she was. The problems are considerable, especially if the father didn't want the separation and feels in no way to blame.

Relationships between child and parent are based on what can be regarded as trivia: 'Did you find the pen you lost?'; 'Are you friends with Chris now?'; 'Did you get your spellings right on Monday?' If there has been a gap of a week or more the child thinks the matter is too small to explain, or the event has been forgotten. But in another sense these are important questions and should be asked because they indicate concern and interest in the child. This is an added hurdle to be overcome in relating to a child who is seen intermittently, because other ways may have to be found to demonstrate to the child that he matters. Children want each parent to be interested in them, and to be fun.

Despite all these difficulties many families do manage to make arrangements which are mutually acceptable, and once the marital hostility has ended then contact meetings become more relaxed and more flexible. There might on occasion be a time for individual children to have Dad's whole attention; flexibility of arrangements helps, especially for an older child, or perhaps a child can take a friend on the visit sometimes. If a father can overcome all the difficulties and continue to have a caring relationship with his child he can take heart. Certainly a relationship of that kind is what a high proportion of children want. When they fill in a sheet asking about 'Your three best wishes', by far the greatest wish is 'To see my dad', or for 'Dad to come home'. Not surprisingly, some research indicated that a high degree of father involvement was an important factor in healthy child development (Kiernan 1991).

## Contact With Fathers

For most children it is important for the non-resident parent to be in contact with the children as soon as possible after the separation, though not all researchers would accept that contact with the father is invariably helpful (Furstenberg and Cherlin 1991).

The opposite view, that only in exceptional circumstances should a child not see the father, is supported by other research, and certainly this is the general opinion in Britain, especially among the judiciary. It is undeniable that the effect on the child of not seeing a parent he loves can have serious long-term consequences, not least because of the feelings of rejection or powerlessness such a decision can raise in the child. Unless the father has harmed his children in some way, is not a good model to emulate, or is unable to relinquish a hostile relationship with his ex-spouse in a way which involves his child, it is usually better for regular contact to be maintained so that the children's security and confidence are not affected adversely, though there are exceptions (see below). It is absolutely right for fathers to have a close relationship with their children provided the relationship is not based on anything other than affection and respect; if it is, it is not likely to be in the child's best interests.

A secret in the background of many divorcing couples is the number of supposed fathers who are not the natural parent of the child. Some have accepted parental responsibility knowing the truth, others are deceived by the mother. Should their rights and responsibilities remain if the truth emerges when the relationship breaks down? And what, morally, should be the position of the true biological father? Harmful investigation is likely to be counter-productive but there are moral dilemmas which are too often ignored. The effect on children of ending a long-term caring relationship can be long-term harm.

Some children have to deal with the aftermath of their parental separation without understanding, the parents being indifferent to their feelings. The hostility continues; Dad, for whatever reason, does not want contact; there are changes of residence, lifestyle; the loss of caring people, and Mum is too depressed to recover quickly. In these families the personality and resilience of the children reinforced by some good experiences, such as support from their siblings or from outside the family, will be crucial for a good outcome.

Another kind of difficulty arises in situations where an absent father has not been in contact with his children for a number of years, sometimes since the time of the separation, then suddenly wants to develop a relationship with them. He may be co-operative and agree to make contact gradually but, not uncommonly, over the years the child has settled in a new family which she finds perfectly satisfactory and has no wish to renew a relationship with a man who, in her eyes, abandoned her. Obviously, there are some good reasons why such a man should get to know his child but, equally, there are those which are not so good. Some of these fathers have had drink or drug problems. When these problems have been resolved, these fathers want a new life which includes their children. Some, because of their circumstances, feel lonely, while others are more concerned to insist on their rights – especially if they are having to pay maintenance.

In examples like this, indirect contact – that is, letters and photographs – may be ordered by the court in the first instance. The effect of this is for the absent parent to resume contact with his ex-spouse, which is an unhappy solution if she is in a stable relationship with a second partner. These situations are almost incapable of a good resolution for everyone.

Perhaps a more frequent situation arises when a child has not been told that the man he believes to be his father is in fact a stepfather. Usually the court advises or orders him to be told as soon as possible. In this situation although the mother might need help in order to handle this delicate matter with sensitivity, it should in most circumstances be remedied as soon as possible, otherwise the child can feel he has been deceived.

Given the many problems and difficulties of parents living apart it seems obvious that, for the sake of the children, some radical changes are needed. In Australia couples sign an agreement to make a long-term commitment to any children, and following the same lines the Institute for Public Policy Research has recently produced a report entitled *A Complete Parent – Towards a New Vision for Child Support* (*Guardian* 7 April 1998). This proposes a contract committing the couple at the time of the marriage to the long-term care of any children they may choose to have. The idea of a Parenting Plan is one which is gaining support.

An important element of the contract is that it would give unmarried fathers more control of and responsibility for their children, which in general is desirable provided the contract can be rescinded if it proves to be not in the best interests of the child at the time of the separation and afterwards, but it could be that abusive fathers will have more rights over the child. This would not be a good solution if at some time in the future emotional abuse and fear are part of parenting and the child's feelings of not wanting to continue contact are ignored. Such a plan might be more child-centred if it was easier to change contact arrangements without incurring financial hardship when they do not appear to be in the best interests of the child.

And what would be in the best interests of the child if parents fail to keep the contract? Enforcement of such a contract might be difficult except in financial matters or in setting standards of care, the breach of which could be detectable by the resident parents, teachers and others in contact with children. These are the kinds of issue mediation meetings should be addressing but which are usually not obvious at the time of separation.

## Returning From Contact Visits

Children can react in many different ways on their return from contact visits. The reasons are complex because strong, conflicting feelings co-exist. Usually they are pleased to be home after an enjoyable time, though for some the pleasure is accompanied by a measure of guilt at having left their Cinderella mother at home; others have enjoyed the visit but are pleased it has ended and they are glad to be home, especially if they have had to behave well all the time.

Regrettably, contact visits frequently have a less agreeable ending. Children can return angry and obstreperous, finding it difficult to un-wind and apparently on course to upset the resident parent with rude-ness and defiance. This behaviour might be interpreted as 'She's so upset on her return, it would be better for her not to go', but this could be an erroneous conclusion. Instead, the behaviour could be related to the child being subjected to remarks during the visit which increase anxiety, or are hostile to the resident parent and make the child feel, because of her dependent needs and vulnerability, unable to deal with the negative comments. Alternatively, having been reminded of her own powerlessness because she is unable to unite her parents, she deals with this uncomfortable feeling by at least ending the contact visit in her own way. She can't do much but she can make the parent she feels safest with angry and in due course be comforted when her tears flow.

Difficult behaviour can also be seen as an expression of anger because of the anxiety caused by awareness of the tension between parents. One parent who took the child to the non-resident parent for a contact visit described it as 'like delivering a bottle of milk'. The child knows from past experience that his parents cannot be civil to each other for long and the situation can soon get out of hand. 'They spoil everything for me', thinks the child. The repeated need to say goodbye is also a source a pain for some, the subsequent parting being a constant reawakening of the first parting, reminding the child of his unhappiness. This is largely ignored, but the frenzied behaviour that may result cannot fail to get a reaction, which, however awful, is better than having to think about the pain inside. 'I'm hurting and I might feel better if I make you hurt too. By my anger I know who I am.'

In short, contact visits are good if they are consistent and reliable and, perhaps most important, free from antagonism. It is the quality of the relationship that matters; whether it is warm and caring, includes some child-centred activities and is based on an understanding of a child's needs. With the child's growing maturity the activities might change emphasis from time to time, but the caring feelings should remain the same.

## Separate Parenting

One of the major tasks for separated parents is that of not showing the children their own feelings about the other parent, even if they are hostile. Another is to try to keep quite separate any conflict which belongs to the relationship with the ex-spouse from their role as parent. It is never helpful to counter the ex-partner's criticism of the other in front of the child because he sees the situation differently and uses different criteria to judge his parents: whether they tell the truth, do what they say they will, are helpful, don't criticize him constantly and never make bad remarks about the other parent, for example. No child wants to hear parents arguing, especially over things which concern him, and especially at the beginning and ending of contact visits and at other flashpoints.

How much does it matter whether the child lives with the mother or father? In practice, it seems, not much for younger boys as long as they have frequent contact with both parents. The quality of parenting appears to be more important than the sex of the resident parent, though some research indicated that children adjust better if custody is with the parent of the same sex (Hetherington 1989). This could be so for older boys, because of being in a male environment or at least having someone to share interests which are primarily masculine. But this is one factor amongst many: the quality of the caring from both parents, other males who are interested in the boy, his temperament and relationship with his mother are some other factors. As most children live with their mother the implication is that boys are less well-adjusted for this reason.

Moreover, as noted earlier, fathers alone often do appear to be more vulnerable and less responsive to feelings than mothers: 'I can't talk to Dad and the only time he talks to me is to shout. He doesn't love me at all.' Fathers who are left by their wives do appear to be susceptible to depression especially if they are not too successful in their new role of single parent.

Two other significant factors should be taken into consideration: which parent the child feels was responsible for the break-up of the marriage, and what age the child is. Thus, a teenager might prefer to live with the parent of the same sex, though there are many exceptions to this and they, like younger children, whether boy or girl, might be happier with the parent they feel closest too, the one who is more loving. Like everything concerned with children of separated parents, there are no easy, straightforward answers.

Sometimes parents attempt to split the caring time equally; for example, one week with Mum and one week with Dad, although even three and a half days with Mum and three and a half days with Dad each week is not unknown. This kind of division is not always success-ful because the child has no fixed base, and what it ignores is the quality of the relationship, which involves sharing the responsibilities and pleasures, and not simply the hours. Teenagers with their complex lives and their need for equipment – which is likely to be in 'the other house' – find this arrangement especially difficult but one that is not easy to change because of the fear of upsetting one of the parents. 'Shared parenting' is more popular in America than Britain, probably because it can seem to parents to be fair, but it is questionable whether all the children involved see it in these terms, or whether it is always in their best interests.

## Children Who Don't Want to See Their Fathers

It is likely that the majority of pre-teenage children who say truthfully and unambiguously that they do not want to see their father have witnessed or experienced violence or abuse; they are frightened of him, and this is a fear which should not be discounted when decisions about arrangements for contact are being made. Without the protection of the resident parent they can be afraid of physical, sexual and emotional abuse. Those who hate, dislike or fear their dad may not wish to see him at all, or want to see him less often than in the existing arrangement; others want to maintain contact but do not want overnight visits.

The argument sometimes put forward for ignoring the child's wish and not taking it seriously is that she will be sorry when older and might then blame her mother for not insisting that contact be maintained. There can be an element of truth in this, especially when, as an adult, there are important occasions which she would like her father to share, such as her wedding or the birth of her first child. But to have a childhood which includes unwanted frequent visits to a man she dislikes or fears at the time is a heavy price to pay for something she might or might not regret in the future. We have no idea how many people there are who, as children, did not want contact and subsequently as adults were sorry to have missed it; it could be surmised that where this does happen their main concern is to please the mother and avoid feelings of divided loyalty.

Older children may have been happy enough to see their father when they were young but as teenagers they are beginning to break away from both parents and lead their own life, and want their changing needs recognized. One fifteen-year-old resented her dad's insistence on taking her to the zoo. His inflexibility over such matters as this and time, caused her to sever the relationship completely after repeatedly trying to explain the difficulties to him.

It is questionable whether subjecting a child to repeated stressful experiences for the adult's benefit is in the child's best interests. What is far more likely is that children want the contact but their fathers no longer do. For different reasons less than half of fathers maintain contact with their children. For some the difficulties of contact were too great in the face of continued marital hostility. Others become involved with new relationships and a new life, and children of the previous relationship could be a reminder of a part of their life which they would prefer to forget. Yet others were never sufficiently interested in their children to make the continued effort that contact requires.

**Parents Who Don't Want Contact**

Children whose parents don't want to see them are often sad children, though some are very angry. Some of the many reasons why parents do not want to continue with the relationship stem from the feelings already referred to, but other are simpler. Fathers can see parenting and marriage as two parts of the same bargain and the logic of this is that parenting ceases when the marriage ends. And it is a regrettable and inescapable fact that some children are not loved by the absent parent. An American research project concluded that the best protection against any adverse consequences of rejection or emotional disturbance is a close relationship with the other parent (Hetherington 1989). The rejection might, during the marriage, have been concealed in order to protect the child from pain.

There was no such sensitivity in either of Michael's parents. He lived with his father, a man who was not happy with the arrangement as Michael was difficult to handle and did not respond to threats of being sent away to be disciplined. The child was restless and had very limited concentration except when given an opportunity to express anger. He said that he wasn't sure whether he wanted to live with his mum, who didn't see him very often, but anyway it wasn't possible because she didn't want him. A child rejected to this extent has to find some physical or behavioural expression for his feeling that neither parent wants him and he believes, as most rejected children do, that it is his fault; nobody wants him because he is naughty. The opposite is the truth; they are 'naughty' because nobody wants them.

Nicola, aged twelve, who lived with her mother, was desperate to see more of her father but knew he didn't like her, preferring her older brother who was an easier child and much more accepting of the situation. Nicola parented her mother, especially when she had been drinking, but despite her daughter's caring her mother continued to make hostile remarks in a joking way about her: 'You can have her, keep her, she is no good.' Nicola said she had no real friends but talked to her dog when she was unhappy. She was a sad child who had had very few good experiences in her life.

Fiona, who was about the same age, also wanted to live with her dad despite having witnessed his frightening violence against her mother. Instead she lived with her mother and stepfather, a disciplinarian who, many times, would send her to bed without food and control her with threats. Again, another child who had little that was good in her life.

This, then, is the dilemma facing courts or mediators. When should a non-resident parent be denied contact with his child? And there is the child's side of the question to be considered – should she have any control over a situation in which one or both of her natural parents do not want to see her? The general assumption is that unless abuse can be proven then the absent parent has a right to continue the

and only in exceptional circumstances should this not be
hild and parent want to see each other and there is no
olution is beyond dispute and it would certainly be in the
nterest to maintain contact. But if the child wants to see a
potenuany harmful parent? The longing for a loving parent can last
many years for children deprived of a relationship they want so much.

This is one of many difficult issues, to which the solution is far
from being clear-cut, especially if the hostility continues and the
mother is undermined and finding it difficult to cope. Research in
America found that any association between the level of contact with a
non-resident parent and children's well-being is weak and that if
conflict is still a major issue, frequent contact is harmful for a child
(Amato and Keith 1991).

## No Contact?

### Emotional Abuse

That children benefit from seeing both parents is a belief which is
generally accepted and for most children this is right and in their best
interests. But setting aside the obvious exceptions where a child is at
risk of physical or sexual harm, there are some grey areas; notably that
of emotional abuse. Its existence is rarely acknowledged, not least
because of the difficulty of proof. Here matters are complicated by an
issue of human rights; are they infringed if parents are stopped from
bringing up a child in the way they think best, provided there is no
obvious abuse?

There are divergent views on the matter, but should a parent who
fails to provide a good model by emotionally harmful or irresponsible
actions forfeit his right? Should the father who tries to remove his
child from school, by force, or the one who wants to take the child to
live abroad, be allowed to continue contact? Should the parent with a
severe drink problem, or one who acts irresponsibly when under the
influence of drugs, have contact? At present the resident parent, aware
of the harmful consequences of such episodes, is likely to be powerless
because of the difficulty of proof. In these circumstances and where
the child has witnessed or been a party to domestic violence, the
child's opinion should contribute significantly to the decision to allow
contact with the abuser to continue.

Emotional abuse is present where there is a sustained attack on the
child's personality through parental belittling of his abilities and
development. It embraces children who are not protected from obvious
danger and those who, when expected to perform tasks quite inappro-

priate to their age, are mocked by parents for their failures. Other abusive demonstrations of parental power include ostracizing just one child and leaving him alone for long periods, teasing unmercifully, or constantly criticizing, so the child becomes the scapegoat of the family. Some use threats: 'I will strangle your mum one day', or 'I will come and take you in the night.' These are verbal manifestations of emotional abuse; other children are imprisoned in their own home, forced to perform demeaning tasks, and so on, by vicious parents. Such children, lacking continuity and care, live in constant fear which could later turn into emotional problems or antisocial behaviour.

Two-year-old Luke's mother left his father after a relationship of fear culminating in a particularly violent episode. Luke's dad, a forceful, bullying man, was given more than average contact by the courts. He desperately wanted his small son to live with him and to this end constantly denigrated the mother to Luke, telling him that his mother was a bad mother who did not really love him and didn't buy him nice things like he did. By the time this little boy was four, he faced a contradiction; should he believe his dad who gave him lovely toys, or should he take notice of how his mother treated him in reality? 'Can you split yourself in two?' he wondered. Not surprisingly, this quite disturbed child had a marked speech problem. This was a harmful contact for which there was no remedy.

Edward, aged four, saw his non-resident father each Wednesday and every other weekend. The father had told his small son he must not tell anyone anything about what they did while they were together. His mother had no idea how he spent his time or what was said to him. Did he feed the ducks, visit his grandparents or go to McDonald's? They were all secrets. We can only guess at the lack of trust in adults this would induce in Edward, and what a strain this imposed silence was on a child who would naturally want to share the good things he had enjoyed. Nor do we know for sure how such a restriction was enforced, or what the father is frightened that Edward might reveal. Four-year-old children still believe in magic, so demons, witches and men from space are real and lions can come in the night and eat you – or eat Mummy.

A damaging restriction of this kind on a very small child and the likelihood that it will have long-term negative consequences may be tantamount to emotional abuse. It is certainly not having the child's welfare at heart by showing understanding and interest and giving encouragement, but is it emotional harm? It is arguable that the phrase 'significant harm' should be widened to include emotional abuse, however difficult this may be to define with any precision.

Parents rarely appreciate how much distress is caused by the constant use of umbrella words such as lazy, selfish, or stupid, or how hurtful it is for a child to be told by her parents that they wished she had never been born. Such children might react aggressively in an attempt to maintain self-esteem, but they are still undermined or may actually come to believe they would be better off dead. Others are used by their parents as if they are adults so that in effect they deny them a childhood. This may be physically, by expecting them to do the household tasks, or emotionally, by using the child as a confidante. Children cannot fail to be affected by receiving these kinds of abuse repeatedly and it is certainly not in their best interests to be exposed to such treatment after separation, when they need extra caring.

The harm done by continued matrimonial hostility has already been mentioned. One striking example was the father who repeatedly told his children that their mother was no good; she was a bad mother and one day he would take the house off her and then the children would have to live with him. This sort of remark tears the children in two and undermines their security. The children, despite loving their father, are likely to be afraid of him and unable to tell anyone what is being said. Likewise, the mother who tells the child that he has a rotten, no-good dad and she wishes he were dead, succeeds in undermining the child's confidence in himself in a way no other comment can. He is, after all, part of this dad, and to rubbish Dad is to rubbish him.

Another child, just five years old and caught up in his parent's hostility, returns from a contact visit in a highly tense state, hitting his head against the wall, saying repeatedly: 'I wish I was dead. I wish I was dead.' It might take an hour to calm him down, but because of fear of or loyalty to his dad he is unable to say what is bothering him. He survives reasonably well because he knows his mum truly loves him. In contrast is a three-year-old also in the middle of terrible hostility between her parents. She is cared for by three different child-minders during the week as both her parents work long hours, then she is 'shared' between two tired parents at the weekend. It is not surprising that she has nightmares, a very poor appetite, and says: 'Mummy doesn't love me; Daddy doesn't love me.' This is an unhappy, deprived child but there are no grounds for stopping her seeing either parent because she wants to see more of both of them, not less.

Current concerns for the rights of a father can sometimes be detrimental if the child's wishes and feelings are ignored. A few parents with defective personalities are so embittered and chaotic and act in bizarre ways or suffer from a mental illness which make them unsuitable to have care of a child, however briefly. They may inflict severe physical punishment, or deprivation. There is a need for clearer guidelines to decide between parental rights and the emotional harm done to a child, without ignoring the wishes and feelings of that child. Supervised contact or short meetings can be possible solutions but need resources which cost money. Because we are so keen that children should see both parents, we can be less concerned about the quality of parenting than we should be.

# 12 Mediation for Parents

## The Present Situation: Divorce

At present the only ground for divorce is irretrievable breakdown. The petitioner has to prove one of five facts: adultery, unreasonable behaviour, a two-year separation with mutual agreement or five years without, or two year's desertion. The person wanting the divorce, the petitioner, has first to consult a solicitor and draw up a Statement of Arrangements covering the future care of the children. This is the only document requiring the approval of both parties. They also have to sign an affidavit to say their statement is true. When arrangements for the children have been agreed, a decree nisi can be granted, followed by the decree absolute six weeks later. The whole process could take a mere three to six months from beginning to end.

The situation will be changed by the Family Law Act 1996 which is currently expected to be implemented in 2000. It states as a guiding principle that when a marriage has broken down the married couple should be encouraged to take all practical steps to save it. If this is not possible the process of ending the marriage should be done with the minimum of distress to the parties and their children, and any risk of violence to a party to the marriage or to any children should, as far as reasonably practicable, be removed or diminished.

The court has to treat the welfare of the child as paramount and in making a decision to postpone the divorce order the court shall have regard to the wishes and feeling of the child and also the conduct of the parties in relation to the upbringing of the child. There is also statutory recognition of the principle that normally the welfare of the child will best be served by having regular contact with both parents and other members of the family.

The Act is concerned to strengthen the institution of marriage by increasing the time divorce takes. It also endorses the expansion of mediation which provides an opportunity for parents to find their own solutions to controversial issues. Although not primarily concerned with children's wishes, the Act reiterates the view that the court must have regard to the wishes and feelings of the child and that it must consider whether it should exercise any of its power under the Children Act in respect of the family. In current mediation practice the expectation is that the parents will interpret and express the child's wishes; where differences cannot be resolved the court will order a court welfare officer to do this, then present a report to the court. However, a number of research projects are taking place at the present time and it is more than likely that when the Act is implemented some major changes will be made.

At present children are invited to attend for a part of a mediation meeting by mediators in some areas. Obviously, this is a way of involving children by giving them the opportunity to be listened to prior to decisions about their future being made, but is hard to imagine that a child will talk freely in front of an unknown mediator and two emotional parents, especially when, as is often the case, they are divided by feelings of loyalty to both parents. Nevertheless, any involvement of children in such an important matter which concerns them is to be welcomed.

## The New Proposals

In outline, three stages are proposed. First, the petitioner is obliged to attend an information meeting; then, after a wait of three months, a statement of marital breakdown, made by one or both parties, has to be filed; following this, for a minimum period of fifteen and a half months, if there are children under sixteen, there is time for reflection and consideration. During this time the couple can receive counselling and/ or mediation which will be voluntary, though there is a monetary consideration. Except where the mediator has grounds for thinking the couple are not suitable for mediation, Legal Aid will not be forthcoming for court proceedings unless mediation has been tried. In the new proposals the quickest divorce will take more than eighteen months if there are children. This increase in the length of time the process will take and the new emphasis on mediation are the two main proposals of the forthcoming Act.

## The Information Meeting

The proposal at present is that when the petitioner wants to divorce he or she will have to attend an information meeting which it is the court's responsibility to provide. This is mandatory, though not for the respondent unless both have filed for divorce. If this is not the case the respondent can attend a separate meeting if he or she chooses. The purpose is to provide information about matters which may arise during the divorce process. Included will be the options available; particulars about marriage counselling and the mediation service; the ways in which children can be helped, and what protection is available concerning violence; information about Legal Aid, and an explanation of the rights each person has.

Three months or more after attending the information meeting a statement of marital breakdown can be filed. It must state that the petitioner or petitioners are aware of the purpose of the period for reflection and consideration and wish to make arrangements for the future. The effect of this is to ensure that any difficulties over property or financial arrangements and those relating to the children are decided before the divorce is granted.

## The Intake Meeting

If mediation is the chosen path for the couple, both of them will be obliged to attend intake meetings which are usually short in duration and always conducted with each partner separately. The aim is to talk about the implications of the service and provide an opportunity to discuss what each partner hopes to achieve. With the mediator, each has to consider whether mediation is a suitable option for them, though it is the mediator who makes the decision.

The meetings, which are the intended precursor to mediation, are likely to be important for obtaining circumscribed information. They have two main purposes: to ascertain whether there is domestic violence or abuse and to decide whether the couple are suitable for mediation. Other difficulties might be revealed at this time, though the division between an intake meeting and mediation must be strictly adhered to. During the course of the meetings the intake officer might elicit important information such as whether either parent has a alcohol or drug problem, or whether there is behaviour in the relationship which causes fear or does harm to spouse or child. The nature of the parenting or any important details regarding the children are less likely to be revealed at these preliminary meetings as the focus is more likely to be on the relationship between the couple.

The intake meeting will be followed by a period for reflection during which the couple will receive counselling and/or mediation if both partners want it. However, where one of the partners does not want mediation, or is not thought to be suitable for it, or where mediation is unlikely to result in an agreement, the court will make a decision on behalf of the couple.

## What Is Mediation?

The first service of the kind, then known as conciliation, was set up in Bristol in 1978, but it is only in the last few years that it has become increasingly accepted as a possible way of intervening when parents divorce or separate. Now called mediation, it is a voluntary service basically concerned to help parents reach a decision over areas of contention regarding the children and is therefore very different from an adversarial system. What takes place in the meetings is legally privileged, though the final outcome can be used in the legal agreement.

In this approach there is an acknowledgement that even though the marital relationship has ended, the parental one has not. The emphasis in matters relating to divorce includes the aim of helping parents negotiate future arrangements *in the best interests of the children*. The meetings are often concerned with matters relating to the non-resident's contact with the children, or other issues which are controversial.

At present, couples are referred for mediation from a number of sources, most often from the courts and solicitors, and a not inconsiderable number are self-referrals. If both agree to attend they are offered an appointment, followed by others if required. Many established centres are becoming affiliated to the National Family Mediation, and consequently their practice at present varies, with some offering one or two meetings, others six or more. It is cheaper than going to court for most people but costs vary; for example, some centres charge £40 per hour, others £75 for a session which could last up to two hours, with a sliding scale in operation. Legal Aid is available for those without resources providing the service meets the criteria laid down by the Legal Aid Board. At present the Board will underwrite the cost of mediation, but the situation is fluid.

Those who are not married and wish to separate can obtain a Judicial Separation for which Legal Aid may be obtainable for matters relating to children.

## Mediation Meetings

Following the intake meetings, and with agreement, couples will be offered joint sessions run by either one or two mediators (again, the practice will vary) who will repeat what the parents have already been told: that the details of the meetings will be treated with confidence unless, subsequently, one or other reveals that a child is being harmed.

In these circumstances the mediation sessions will be postponed pending enquiries by a social services department. Normally, at the conclusion of the sessions couples will agree to a brief summary of the decisions made, copies of which will be given to them, the court and their solicitors. The decisions are not legally binding until the solicitor has presented them to the court and the court has approved them.

At present, different practices are in operation: some units have one mediator conducting the interview with another in the role of a supervisor; others have two mediators conducting the interview jointly; or, in a way more usual in the United States, one will interview and the other watches behind a screen and interrupts from time to time. Some services include the children for much of the time, others merely bring them in to share the parental decision, and a small number do not see them at all. Some have a policy of never leaving the couple alone together; others frequently do so for perhaps ten minutes to give either the couple or themselves a breathing space, or time to discuss an issue.

The information discussed at the intake meeting will be reinforced, and the couple given some practical details about the length of the meeting and other relevant matters. It can be useful for the mediator to share what little he or she knows about the family at the beginning of mediation.

Then it is necessary to discuss the problem of how each of them sees it. What solutions have been tried? What did they both do to try and solve it? When did it begin? Is anyone else involved with the problem; if so, what do they do? It is important to hear exactly what parents want because conducting interviews at such an emotional time may result in the participants not being as clear or articulate as they would otherwise be, therefore assumptions that may be hidden in their statements should be clarified.

The mediator has to be as impartial as possible, something which can be difficult if one partner is more verbal or forceful than the other. If there is a danger of this not happening the mediator can ask the couple to remind him. Underlining all the interventions is the rule that parents must make the decisions – it is their problem; the mediator is the facilitator. Mediators are not therapists. Therapy focuses on feelings. Can you say more about how you felt then? How was it for you? Why do you think so-and-so did that? In contrast, mediation is more likely to put the emphasis on actions. What did you do when he said that? What happened next? How would she know you love your son? What could he do to reassure you that your child will be safe with him? By getting a picture of how the couple talk to each other, the relationship between them becomes clearer. But each mediator will develop his or her own style, and focus on what is perceived as important. For them to give advice or even to make suggestions, however indirect they appear to be, is not permitted; rather the mediator is concerned to enable the couple to find their own solution to disputes.

## Mediators and Training

The National Family Mediation, already referred to, is a growing nation-wide body involved in the training which leads to mediators becoming affiliated members and thereafter subject to regular assessment. They are not legally trained, many having come from the probation or similar services.

Until comparatively recently there have been different practices, though with the present emphasis given to mediation, there is likely to be an increase in uniformity as well as in the number of centres throughout the country. This will lead to a more professional service, something which is not possible or indeed desirable until different approaches have been tried and their results evaluated. Research into these matters is taking place at present. One important development is the setting up of the UK College of Family Mediators, which has the aim of promoting standards and training, creating codes of practice and putting in place complaints procedures. Six bodies are affiliated, including the Family Mediators Association and National Family Mediation.

One form of this work is known as All Issues Mediation in which mediators are trained to discuss matters relating to financial matters, property and children's issues. They work with the couple in twos, one of whom will be an experienced family solicitor and the other an experienced mediator. They might, for example, assist parents to come to a decision about where a child should live or help them over property or financial matters. All are members of the Family Mediators Association and are not authorized to advise or represent either party individually. A summary of any proposed agreement would need to be taken to solicitors to be formalized and presented to the court. The mediators will not give advice themselves but may suggest that the couple consult their own solicitors if no consensus is reached.

## Court Intervention

At present, most couples do not want to be involved in the mediation process, preferring instead a court order, though agreements based on parental participation and compromise are more likely to last than if the court has made the decision. Amongst the reasons why parents do not want mediation can be that they feel deeply wronged and want this acknowledged publicly; in other words they want 'their day in court'. Others feel that because there is so much hostility in their relationship they are reluctant even to sit in the same room as their ex-spouse. It is the fear of not feeling safe enough to discuss matters which influences them and can be the reason for not wanting this type of intervention. Some parents who are very conscious of their lack of verbal skills and consequently expect to be at considerable disadvantage in mediation meetings prefer the matter to be dealt with by solicitors and other legally trained experts.

The Family Law Act proposes that to be represented in court Legal Aid will no longer be available for those who qualify unless mediation has been tried first, though there are some exceptions. A mediator or person conducting the intake meeting might consider mediation unsuitable for a number of reasons; there might be too much hostility between the couple or domestic violence or child abuse has taken place during the partnership, though if both partners want mediation and the mediator agrees, this may not necessarily be a bar.

If, after mediation, the couple cannot agree about the future arrangements for the child and there is no satisfactory outcome, the court is likely to order a welfare report. Then, in due course, a court welfare officer will see the child alone and with both parents separately, as well as interviewing others who are important to the child or involved with him. The welfare report is then submitted to the court, part of a long process which gives a picture of the family and child to the court, who then may recommend a course of action after exploring the various options. In these circumstances the decision then is no longer in the hands of the parents.

## Advantages of Mediation

Mediation has a number of advantages over the court in making decisions concerning the children: court officials and mediators alike attempt to be impartial, but in mediation parents have some control. Any agreement arrived at is based on compromise, both parents stating what they think would be the best arrangement for themselves and for the children now and in the future, therefore they are not concerned to be as negative as they can about their partner, but rather become aware that it is in their own interests to present themselves in a good light.

In mediation, assessing blame is not relevant. It is likely to be better for children because in the adversarial system each party is concerned to show the other as badly behaved or as irresponsible as possible, the very opposite to compromise. Hard words said in court can be like very deep wounds and add to the disharmony between the couple. In addition, and in contrast to an adversarial system, one consequence can be improved communication between the parents. Small incidents are less likely to be enlarged into big issues, and it is possible that there could be some acceptance that they could have played some part in the breakdown of the relationship. This is a better outcome than having to deny even the smallest degree of responsibility.

There is the likelihood that other benefits can be gained from mediation. Because parents are asked what they think would be best, they retain some control and self-esteem, and one benefit can be that they learn to negotiate, knowledge which may be useful for the future. It is a time of emotional turmoil but, if the partners can use their reasoning as well as their feelings, they may be helped to move from their entrenched positions to seeing their situation differently, leading to a successful outcome.

Antagonism expressed in mediation meetings can be a way of hiding some unacceptable feelings which are difficult to face. But some parents, especially fathers, see the meetings as a second chance, a way of compensating for failures as a parent in the past, and a chance as a lone parent to start again. The child's perception might not be the same to begin with until there is a realization that there has been a change for the better, and they are loved and valued.

Another consideration is that it is arguably a cheaper alternative than a court order, in part because of the cost of solicitors and barristers; Legal Aid is not available for those with resources above a certain level (at present those with a disposable income of over £80 per week do not qualify) and those who have assets worth more than £2,500 will have to pay the money back. In addition, for everyone a court appearance is time-consuming and stressful.

## Limitations of Mediation

There are some serious limitations. No marital relationship is equal; both parties have areas where, probably in very subtle ways, each is more powerful than the other, but in families where the inequality is a result of fear, mediation as the best way of proceeding is open to question. Mediation can exacerbate the difficulties or condone the inequality if this is not realized. Much of the control by fear is implicit, known only to the victim, and there are areas which are too explosive to risk in mediation meetings. Perhaps feelings are running too high, or one or both parties have little control over their behaviour or are not interested in discussion and compromise. Where there is domestic violence this may be more obvious than when control is by subtle bullying or verbally induced fear. Timing, too, can be relevant; mediation meetings can be arranged too soon after the separation when emotions are too raw or the pain is too severe at that time for a successful outcome, though of course the proposed intake meetings will help to delay the start.

Not all of those concerned are in favour of mediation as presently conceived, primarily because it is not concerned with preventative actions. A four-year follow-up of the effect of mediation in Newcastle (Walker 1993) showed little evidence that mediation focussed on children resulted in long-term benefits. The conclusion was that mediation does not attempt to deal with trauma and shows no appreciation that anger and conflict are endemic to the process of marital separation. In addition, the psychological processes underlying divorce are largely ignored by lawyers.

In contrast, a more recent survey (McCarthy and Walker 1996) found that two-thirds of clients were satisfied with mediation, and the same proportion felt the meeting had helped them reduce conflict. Six out of ten had reached an agreement over the children, though one-quarter did not reach any agreement. This report gives a positive picture of the advantages of this way of working, including improved communication, a reduction of bitterness and tension and enhanced negotiating skills, to the benefit of the children.

It has been argued that some parents are concerned to come to an agreement which might suit them, but which is not in the best interests of the child. Nevertheless, despite these anxieties it is usually a better option for the parents than resorting to the courts, though this route will be more appropriate for some couples because of the nature of the marital relationship – when, for example, a mother and child need protection, or a father feels very strongly that he would be the best parent to care for the children and wants his point of view expressed by a person trained in legal matters.

In a number of selected areas trials which are in operation, experimenting with some of the proposals, may result in modifications when the Act is implemented.

## Mediation and Domestic Violence

Whether mediation is possible if domestic violence is involved is an issue under discussion. Some mediators believe that women are not truthful or exaggerate the incidents, and thus they doubt the extent of violence; others are convinced, accepting studies which show many women are victims and that there is a link between domestic violence and the abuse of children. The Women's Aid Federation, as a result of its research, has no doubt that the prevalence of domestic violence is a contributory factor in a large number of marriage breakdowns. It is also reported to increase at the time of separation (Hester and Pearson 1993). If one partner is frightened it is not likely that she will be able to negotiate in the best possible way on her own behalf; protecting herself from possible future hurt will dominate her thoughts. The imbalance of power is inevitable if domestic violence has been a part of the marital relationship, and there is a serious risk of mediation adding to the harm done by condoning the situation. This raises doubts whether mediation is the best way of proceeding in these circumstances.

Where children are not involved in the mediation meetings, or are invited to part of a session to hear the results of the negotiations, the mediator will have to rely on the parents' perceptions of the children and their needs, without hearing from the children themselves. The mediator therefore has to make sure children's views are to the forefront and their well-being is not forgotten. In this connection he or she will need to have some idea of the history of each and of the relationships in the family before possible options can be discussed. It may be necessary to help parents ascertain their children's views without bias, always remembering that each child can have a different view about what he or she wants, even quite young ones. The children would have to understand that it is important for parents to know what they feel even though they, the parents, will make the decisions.

## Some Parental Patterns

A not uncommon situation occurs when the parents have separated but are still emotionally involved with each other. 'An unconsummated divorce' is a phrase which has been used in these circumstances. Mediators have to be alert for signs that the child is being used in this unfinished business. Has Dad got a new car? Where's he going for his holiday? Does he talk about me? What's Mum's boyfriend like? Does he take her out a lot? Does she talk about me?

Some ex-partners want to finish completely with everything associated with their failed marriage. Others want to end the marriage but not the relationship. For them the problem may be not having the social skills to make the break, even though this is what is wanted. They fear the result will be that they will be out-manoeuvred and end up feeling they have lost. More aggressive people keep the relationship going because they know the ex-partner is annoyed or upset by their constant intrusion and demands. Those who are more fearful might be frightened of the unforeseen consequences, or perhaps of being lonely. One dad said his children had to get used to his having left the family home gradually; he insisted on returning to them each weekend and behaving as if he had not left and no divorce was underway. In reality he couldn't end the relationship with his wife, however acrimonious it was. He feared the future would be too bleak without the endless battles.

Sometimes the only way forward is for the mediator to put fears resulting from this kind of situation into words, to be considered openly. Other separated parents find that it is not easy to end a relationship which lacks any warmth with a partner, while continuing to love and have concern for a child of the relationship. To discuss this honestly can be a first step towards a better relationship with the ex-partner and towards a more satisfactory conclusion to mediation.

It might be helpful if some important details of the family background are discussed, but information of this kind is not thought to be relevant at present. Its desirability does not accord with the views of National Family Mediation where the focus is on the present and the future, not the past. As has been said before, unresolved emotional difficulties from the past can jeopardize future relationships. They can play a large part in unhappy marriages and overshadow the good experiences.

A wife who had an unstable childhood, having been cared for by different people, and grew up feeling uncertain and doubtful of her abilities to sustain relationships, had all the old feelings awakened when her husband told her he was going abroad for the weekend to watch football with his mates. The husband, who had also experienced self-doubt because of his unhappy childhood, might have had a problem because his wife said she must see her mother every day. A mediator would not be concerned to understand the reasons for the strength of emotions over what might be seen as a fairly trivial matter.

An understanding of such patterns can provide powerful determinants in how the divorce or separation might be handled. Failure to do so could result in an agreement which will not have a satisfactory outcome in the long term. In the example above, both expected to meet the other's emotional needs; their partner's wish to share them with others was too hard to accept. But these unresolved feelings can also affect the couple in mediation meetings. The hurt at what was felt as rejection is dealt with by wanting to hurt back, wanting revenge, a situation which can easily involve the children because the previous flashpoints are not known.

What actually happened when one partner left the family home can also give clues about the couple's personalities. Many couples have had a number of separations before the permanent one, and with growing discontent the separation was expected. Parents who are concerned about the effect on the children might plan the separation, choosing the best moment, deciding how they will tell the children and working out some of the details before the event. In contrast, some separations occur at the height of a row when tempers flare, which is perhaps the worst scenario for the children; more than one mother has thrown her husband's clothes and belongings out of the bedroom window. What did the remaining partner do? How did it end? The effect of not having a proper ending can affect future patterns of relationship between the couple, especially if there are hurt feelings which have not been expressed or have been hidden by anger.

This introduces one of the present dilemmas of mediation; where does mediation end and counselling begin? If a mediator is aware of these underlying feelings which have such a powerful influence on behaviour, can he or she ignore this knowledge? The thinking at present is that the mediator must, because such analysis is irrelevant to the mediation process and there have to be boundaries, especially when a new discipline being established.

At present, the focus of mediation is often on helping the parents to reach a compromise over a particular issue – the duration of a contact meeting for example, or whether it should take place weekly or every other week. This, of course, can be very important if parents have been unable to agree to anything for years, and is the best we can do at present, but, in the long term, is it enough? Because of the potential harm divorce can cause children, should the mediation service have any responsibility for attempting to reduce marital breakdown? Is it enough for the mediator to feel: 'Oh good, they came to an agreement about contact', or is this just the beginning?

If a different approach was accepted it would raise another serious problem. What sort of training would be appropriate for mediators if there is seen to be a need for considering relevant family history? Such changes would have to wait until mediation is more popular and more widely used than at present. In addition more financial help would need to be available, and greater demands for ongoing supervision met.

Mediation, as currently perceived and practised, is limited largely to problems outstanding after separation and which affect the ex-partners and their children. Obviously, to have the opportunity to 'think aloud' about outstanding areas of conflict, and perhaps see them in a different way, can be immensely helpful. But should more be incorporated in mediation? Should there be a wider approach to include long-term consequences; for instance, helping the couple deal with their anger, or helping them look at the patterns which have affected the marriage so that if they engage in another relationship there is less danger of their repeating the mistakes of the first? A big bonus for the children involved would be their being cared for by more successful parents.

An ongoing scientific analysis of this approach would need to be built in, techniques improved and the limitations of mediation addressed. As in all professions, mediation is only as good as its practitioners. But this is a new discipline, and there is much to organize in providing a uniform service with high standards. These are questions for the future, when, it is to be hoped, children will be the prime consideration.

# 13 Children and Mediation

## Should Children Be Involved?

There are conflicting views about whether children should be involved in the mediation process, ranging from their total exclusion to full participation. The National Family Mediation's journal, *Family Mediation*, provides a focus for discussion and for the presentation of the organization's thinking. Only very recently has it become more sympathetic to involving children.

The first view is that children should not be involved at all and that the mediators should learn about their wishes via the parents. Those who take this position believe parents are the best people to make decisions on behalf of their children and about the post-marriage situation overall, which includes making acceptable arrangements for them. The National Family Mediation guidelines (April 1996) expressed the view that this method, which it referred to as indirect consultation, is the preferred practice because it encourages parents to consider their children's views and reinforces their right to make decisions on their behalf. While this may be true as long as a marriage is functioning well, unfortunately, at such a time of stress and parents' views are not always reliable and can be conflicting.

The time immediately after the decision to divorce is highly charged emotionally and parents may not have actually found out what each individual child feels and wishes. Parents involved in conflict are too immersed in their own distress and anger to put this aside and discuss rationally with the children important issues which will affect them directly. Obviously, many do know what each child wants and they agree about what would be best. Those who don't and present conflicting views in mediation meetings, might be encouraged to discuss the matter with the children, bearing in mind that they often welcome the opportunity to express their views but do not want to make decisions or choose between parents.

As has already been said, in a very few areas children are usually not present. Bristol Family Mediation Service has expressed a firm opinion that 'to promote the interests and well-being of the children is best done by empowering parents, not seeing children'. In their view mediation is about helping parents come to a decision, though even that uncompromising statement can find an exception if circumstances demand it and the mediator agrees their presence would serve a useful purpose. A further point in favour of this view is that where parents have been unable to reach an agreement and the antagonism which really belongs to the marriage continues unabated, children should not be present. It may, of course, be more of a worry to the mediators, because for the children this is familiar parental behaviour. There is also a fear that involving them may undermine the authority of parents and therefore it should not be encouraged.

The first alternative view is that children, with their own and their parents' agreement, should be invited to see a mediator on their own, with the mediator then reporting back to the parents at a mediation meeting. National Family Mediation refers to this method as direct consultation. If the children are being seen separately they have to have trust in the mediator to convey to parents their wishes and feelings in the most helpful way possible, and that what they say will be reported to their parents accurately. Their wish not to have some of the comments repeated is usually respected. In other words, they have the opportunity to say what they think and believe it is safe to reveal, while knowing that some of what they say will be conveyed to their parents. In addition, out of the current sixty-seven National Family Mediation centres in existence, counselling for children is currently available in about twenty (January 1999).

Greater involvement of children is apparent in a second alternative, to include the children in some of the meetings with the parents. This is not generally favoured by National Family Mediation, though if the mediator agrees, their policies allow for children to be present for feedback, to join in a limited discussion or to be told of the parenting plan. It is the practice in some mediation centres to include the children in the mediation meetings with the parents, but only if the mediator thinks this would be helpful and parents and children agree. A number of centres already invite children to at least one session, others to part of a session, while yet others believe that they should be seen only at the mediator's discretion. In other words, practice varies and thinking is fluid, though increasingly children are involved to some extent.

Another possibility is for mediation to be child-focused; it is a good experience for children to know their parents are listening to what they say and so they may, for the first time, become aware of the children's distress and the chasm between how they see the situation compared with the way the children see it. Just to be listened to is valuable for children, as it is valuable for them to know what is happening, whatever the outcome. They can benefit, too, from the experience of their parents' trying to find a solution which would be right for them, especially when the latter, following separation, have been absorbed in their own feelings. They can find the meetings a safe place to express what they could not say at home and also can be reassured that the separation was not their fault, and that it is all right to be sad or angry. One mediation centre stated forthrightly: 'Our policy is based on the premise that divorce is a time of family stress and mediation is more likely to be successful if children have a voice in this process' (Herefordshire Family Mediation 1996). To listen to children is in line with the UN Charter and the Children Act 1989.

When children are present they should be encouraged to express openly their worries and difficulties while parents listen. The main purpose of involving them has to be clearly stated. It may be because it is felt important for them to have an opportunity of saying what they think, but they must be told clearly that they cannot make decisions – this is the task of parents who are trusted to do so with the best interests of the children in mind. It will also be necessary to state clearly the exceptions to maintaining confidentiality.

Some clear ground rules are required when children attend with their parents. The first is that parents have to appreciate that the meeting is concerned with them as parents, not as spouses, and it is not beneficial for the children to hear their recriminations; therefore they must not argue or shout in front of them. Other rules are that the children can leave the meeting if they want to and parents have to agree to listen to them; and a rule for the mediator should be that the meeting must end at the time agreed. If a meeting carries on it shows that the mediator is not in control. If more time is needed a further meeting can be arranged.

The debate about including children is reminiscent of the long drawn-out discussions many years ago about whether fathers should be invited to what were then called Child Guidance Clinics. A father was not at that time considered relevant to a meeting about his child who was causing concern. Until this matter was resolved, only the mother and child were seen, usually separately and only together at the end of the session to hear what the plan would be – a meeting which would now be called 'feedback'. In contrast, twenty years later some clinics, endorsing Family Therapy wholeheartedly, went through a phase of not making appointments unless the father agreed to be present.

## Children in Meetings

Some children are able to express themselves well in front of a person they don't know, though experience in running children's groups (where confidentiality is paramount) suggests that it is not until at least the third or even the last meeting that most children feel safe enough and acquire the courage to express their truer feelings and deep-seated worries, a view that can be confirmed by any counsellor or therapist. It is possible that in mediation such quite fleeting contacts with children, at a time of anxiety and stress for the child, are not always as successful as intended. Disclosures made in these circumstances are capable of leaving the child with powerful guilt feelings and can be harmful.

Children who are overwhelmed with anxiety and believe they must protect the more vulnerable parent are unable to state their feelings straightforwardly. They find it difficult to do so because of their ambivalence about the situation. This is because their emotions are a compound of loving and hating, feeling good about being needed and bad about resenting the pressures put on them, fear of something terrible going to happen and anger that their caring is causing confusion. Underlying all these can be the fear that, because of other changes beyond their control, they might end up with neither parent wanting them. They feel caught in an impossible situation which compels them to remain silent and distressed.

But it is impossible not to communicate, and even these unexpressed feelings have to be respected. In this situation, parents, because they are embarrassed by their child's behaviour, tend to start nagging: 'Say something then, this is why we have brought you here. Have you lost your tongue, or what?' If two or three sessions with the child alone were planned, it might be possible to help her to communicate her feelings to the parents and thereby encourage the parents to listen. In most circumstances this would be less destructive.

Many children are brought up by those who think parenting is basically about obedience and believe that parents have to demonstrate they are in charge. As a result they have little experience of discussing even small issues with their children. How can we expect children like these, who have never had the experience of being asked what they think or want and have been unused to having control over even trivial matters, to be able to express their views about a highly emotive subject such as their future to strangers and in front of parents, neither of whom they want to offend? This is not an argument for not involving children, rather for seeing them a few times to encourage a feeling of trust. They might then feel able to express their true opinion.

Joe was asked by a court welfare officer (who should have known better) to say which parent he wanted to live with, but for him there was no clear-cut answer. He loved both Mum and Dad, though he hated the children of Mum's partner. But his younger sister was going to live with Mum and he loved her. On the other hand, Dad was on his own and Joe knew that if he, his only son, said he wanted to live with Mum, Dad, who wasn't managing very well, would be deeply hurt. He said: 'With the brain of a thirteen-year-old, I can't sort this out.'

One way out of dilemmas of this kind is for the child to take sides, but probably the majority try to maintain a relationship with both parents. 'She cries when she has to go and see him and when he comes home she is tense and difficult', says her mother. 'That's rubbish,' says her father, 'she loves every moment she is with me and cries when she has to leave. She says she wants to come and live with me when she is bigger.' It is quite likely that both parents are speaking the truth. The child is enjoying a loving relationship with both parents but, because of her being so much aware of their antagonism towards each other and her anxiety about their continuing to love her, she has no alternative but to imitate the negative feelings each partner has for the other. A mediator may find it difficult to appreciate the child's predicament by only talking to her parents.

Children are not usually invited to the first meeting because it is important to discuss the possibility of the children being present at future meetings, if the mediator thinks it would be desirable, and both parents and children agree to their being involved. At the first meeting mediators can also gain some idea of the areas of dispute between the parents. This involves attempting to understand the feelings underlying the statements. A mum might say: 'Of course I want them to see their dad', but the unspoken thought is 'I don't really, though I know they should, but life is easier for him than for me and before long the children might prefer to live with him and his new partner and I don't want this to happen.' A dad might say: 'Of course I want to see them, I'm their dad', but his unspoken thought is: 'Yes I do in a way but it's difficult amusing them for such a long time and if I didn't I would be very lonely and anyway I know my ex-wife would rather I kept right away.' Such complex thoughts show that it is normal for parents to have mixed feelings as well as the children. Obviously, it helps if mediators have some understanding of these, but although they do not give advice and should not even make suggestions, such awareness can't fail to influence them.

The mediator can reinforce the parents' role but is also able to provide an opportunity for them to talk about events which they find painful or which can arise from their own guilt about the part they played. This can help the children to realize that they were not responsible for the break-up. Another advantage is that the parents might learn from the mediators the technique of giving complete attention to a child by active listening and respecting what the child says. The father who told his daughter she was 'as thick as two planks' when trying to help her with homework, and the mother who repeatedly prophesied that her son would 'turn out bad, just like his father', might benefit from being exposed to a different model of parenting than their existing one.

The advantage for the mediator of having face-to-face contact with the children in the family lies in gaining a clearer understanding of each one. It also demonstrates an awareness that the child is a member of a family group who contributes both to the events which affect the family and to making them happen, or not. This is true whether the family is headed by one parent or two. Everybody is affected by everybody else; to see two family members and ignore the others when such an important issue is being discussed, one which affects them all, is likely to result in an outcome that is not as good as it might be.

But a word of caution: when seeing children alone, in groups or in mediation meetings, it is always important for those conducting the interview to keep in mind the effects of their intervention. As was said in discussing the role of counsellors, the mediator must also avoid falling into the trap of being the ideal understanding parent. The consequence of such a fantasy is to undermine a parent's ability to parent a child and that in the end the child has to deal with another harmful event, that of an adult they thought they were special to, rejecting them at the end of the sessions. 'She's nicer than you, I bet she wouldn't make me go to bed so early. I wish she was my mum.'

**The Relevance of a Child's History**

In this and the following section a number of the wider issues concerning children with separated parents will be discussed. The first relates to the often repeated phrase used by writers, researchers and practitioners that 'divorce is a process' – a valuable idea, but unfortunately one which is often ignored in mediation. In meetings the emphasis is on the present and the future. It is not thought necessary to discuss the past, yet the history of the family is likely to be highly relevant, and to exclude the pre-divorce relationships between the child and both parents is open to question and cannot always be in the child's best interests.

One small girl was virtually ignored when her brother was born. Her distress at such rejection was expressed by 'bad' behaviour. When, subsequently, her parents divorced she was thought to be reacting to this event, whereas in fact family work showed it was the experience which had begun four years previously, and was continuing, which caused her unhappiness. The proposed intake meetings could avoid such erroneous conclusions by collecting helpful background information which would make it possible to assess the situation more accurately, but this would require a drastic change from what is proposed at present.

Nina's early experience played a very important part in her development. Her parents had separated a few months after her birth. When she was fifteen months old, Mrs Brown, her mother, had to stay in hospital for more than two weeks. Against the mother's wishes the baby was cared for by the paternal grandparents, people Nina did not know well and who decided it would be better if she did not see her mother during this time.

When Mrs Brown recovered and returned home, the grandparents, with the agreement of Nina's father, insisted that her mother was not well enough to care for her daughter; this, despite Mrs Brown's protests and those of Nina's maternal grandmother, who had always been involved with her granddaughter and was able and willing to care for both mother and baby daughter in their own home. When, after a number of weeks and a great deal of unpleasantness, the little girl did come home, not surprisingly she was very clinging and upset, and although she recovered from the experience in time, it left deep scars of insecurity.

When Nina's father remarried he insisted on having his now four-year-old daughter for three nights every other weekend. The arrangements were made without any consideration of the child's feelings and led to the old wounds reopening so that once again she showed signs of distress and anxiety. She started wetting her bed again, developed sleeping problems and lost interest in her usual activities. These feelings, in time, turned to anger against her mother for making her see her father, though Mrs Brown believed she had no choice.

The importance of the trauma of the early separation had never been appreciated and could have resulted in long-term harm had it not been for the love, understanding and stability her mother and maternal grandmother gave her. Fortunately for Nina, her father and his new wife had a baby and from that time he did not need his elder child as a pawn in his anger with his ex-wife, and a rather more positive relationship could develop. If this sort of background is not known it is unlikely that the best solution for children will be found, especially if, as in this family, the father is a successful businessman who can be charming and persuasive.

When the focus of the meetings is the issue of contact it is worth questioning whether it really is in the best interests of the child, something which cannot be answered without finding out something of the child's background. This involves getting a picture of the family before separation which will include the quality of family relationships, and the kind of parenting which the child has experienced. A child who has had long-term inadequate parenting which continues after separation has a different problem from one whose parenting was satisfactory but has declined since the split. Only when these aspects are known can there be some understanding of whether the child is reacting primarily to the separation and the emotional turmoil surrounding it, or whether the behaviour and anxiety are consequences of long-term difficulties. Depending on the circumstances, there are important questions the mediator ought to bear in mind. What violence has the child witnessed or been a part of? Is there any history of neglect? Has the child experienced a loving, caring relationship from either or both parents? Is the child enjoyed? Was this a largely absent parent for whatever reason?

## Eliciting Information

It is possible and desirable to discover other information relating to the separation in a more indirect way than is indicated here. It is unlikely that there were no changes in behaviour, but it might be informative to know what parents had noticed. Some of the changes might be very small but nevertheless can be significant.

To elicit details of the actual separation can be enlightening; for example, by discovering when the separation took place, how old the children were, who told them and what was said. How did each one react – the same or differently? Following the separation, was there a change in behaviour? Were the parents aware of the children's sadness? Were symptoms such as a return to a previous stage of development, or sleeping difficulties, apparent? This sort of information would indicate something about the child's feelings for both parents and his reactions and resilience.

A picture of the current child–parent relationship, which could have altered considerably, might also help towards producing a good outcome for the children, the details of which have been discussed. Questions, which will have to be framed in an indirect way, may include: Are parents aware of the different needs of each child in the family depending on their ages, personality and relationships? What do they think the effect of their anger might be on their child? Are they successful at containing their feelings about each other whatever the provocation? How concerned are they about the child's progress at school? A dad who does not hear his young child read but leaves it to his new girlfriend is a source of considerable resentment for a number of children. Through all these questions it will be possible to answer another: does this parent make the child feel loved and special and meet his or her emotional needs? This approach, using rather more penetrating comments, would emphasize the emotional content of the parent–child relationship.

Information about the situation at the time of the meeting would include parents' feelings about issues which concern the children, such as the frequency of contact meetings and the degree of flexibility as well as the arrangements for overnight stays and holidays, especially for young children. How were these decisions arrived at? Which of them are parents not happy about? Which are the children not happy about? In the short proposed intake meeting where the issue of safety is of primary importance there will not be time to discuss them in any depth.

Because they are not generally thought of as relevant, the answers to these questions are not usually known at present, but if finding what is in the best interests of the child is to be more than a empty phrase, discussion of them is important. Even one meeting which includes such topics can be helpful, particularly since the emphasis has to be on helping parents find their own solution to their problems.

The child-centred approach suggested is radically different from those proposed in the forthcoming Family Law Act. It would be expensive in the short term and would require more resources, but the benefits to the great number of children involved in acrimonious divorces could be considerable.

## Conclusion

Despite some fairly serious criticisms of mediation, for many of those who use the service the gains can be considerable, especially if parents know how each child in the family feels about arrangements which affect them and each one's opinions are sought and treated seriously. The forthcoming legislation which advocates mediation contains good ideas, but the fundamental conflict of aims is contradictory: to maintain the family as an institution is confused with the desire to reduce the number of divorces by making them more difficult to obtain.

The compromise contains many fine words and concepts but overlooking the expertise and resources needed to put them in place. There are a number of missed opportunities – especially regarding the children whose interests are secondary to the emphasis on the attempt to save marriages and to alter the procedures of divorce for parents. It is to be hoped that at least some of the inconsistencies will be addressed when the Act is fully operational.

In view of the very long delay and the complications proposed, it would be ironical if an Act whose rationale is to save marriages, has the effect of increasing the number of couples who choose to cohabit rather than to marry, in order to avoid the possibility of experiencing the difficulties of divorce.

# 14    A Chapter Addressed to Children Whose Parents Don't Live Together

This chapter is for you if you are a child or young person who feels confused or upset because your parents have separated, whether it was recently or a long time ago. It may help you to see things differently, and the hope is that it could help you feel better. It's written as if your dad has left and you are living with your mum, because that's how most children are placed; but I know some children live with their dad and if you are one, please read 'dad' instead of 'mum' because it is clumsy to write 'your dad or your mum' each time.

## Marriage and Separation

Parents who separate are like everyone else, except they were unlucky and, despite the good things, such as having children, the happiness they wanted and expected when they got married did not last. Usually the break-up was not the fault of one person only but the result of lots of things, often over many years, that went into making the marriage unhappy. In fact, it is not helpful for you to think in terms of whose fault it was.

When people get married they want important things like being loved and feeling special. It is difficult for everyone to achieve a happy marriage and if many quite small things start to go wrong there can be problems. When this happens, hurt and anger start to take the place of love.

Before they separate most parents try hard to make their marriage successful, but it is when they reach the point of seriously wondering if the family would be happier if they lived apart, that they think of divorce. Sometimes one of them has met someone else whom they think will make them happy, but not always.

There is likely to be anger and sadness in the family, especially if, as is often the case, only one parent wanted the divorce. But in time, their feelings change (as yours do) and the anger and sadness become less important. Fortunately, after a time, which may be a year or two, most parents stop being upset; they accept the situation and see the future with hope.


## Some Feelings You Might Have

Divorce usually means big changes for children and a lot of uncertainty about what is going to happen. If you feel like this, you might find you have different feelings at the same time or you might be among the few children who, at the start of the separation, feel all right about parents divorcing, believing it is the best thing which could happen to the family. But many are *sad* because a parent is living somewhere else and is missed a lot. If you feel like this then it's all right to cry, through it is probably best if you do so at home or when you are with people to whom you are close.

You might feel upset and *hurt* or *betrayed*. 'How could they do this to me?' It can be easy to forget that they might be thinking of you because they know that for you the rows between them are upsetting, but also they are separating in the hope that everyone will be happier. Sometimes you might feel that you are *different* from other children; perhaps you do not want to do things you used to enjoy, or you have a problem concentrating at school. You may feel, like many children, *less confident* and, because you are sad and worried, can feel your friends do not like you.

You may feel *angry*, which is an ordinary human emotion like happiness, sadness, fear or love. This may be about lots of things such as having parents who won't listen to you, or won't tell you what is going to happen, or sheer frustration at not being able to prevent what you know is happening. The task is not to keep your anger bottled up – that's harmful, but you have to find a way to show it which doesn't hurt you or other people. But remember that nobody knows the feelings inside your head – unless you tell them.

Quite often children feel *powerless* because they have to accept that they can't make happen what they really want to happen. This gets better when they realize that there are some good things about the separation for them. Feeling *frightened* or *anxious* can have many different causes, one of the commonest being not knowing what changes are going to take place. And of course, like a lot of children you may be *worried* about your future. Will you have an unhappy marriage? If there has been violence in your family could you grow up to be violent? If you are thinking about these things it means that they are much less likely to happen.

Being *puzzled* or *confused,* wondering who is right and who is wrong, might also be familiar to you. One parent says this; the other says the opposite – who will you believe? If parents haven't always told the truth or are keeping secrets from you, then you might feel angry too. Sometimes they do this because they are embarrassed; sometimes they think they are protecting you from painful feelings, and sometimes they do not understand how important it is to tell you the truth so that you don't lose your trust in them and what they say. If you don't know what will happen, let alone why it is happening, it can be difficult to ask questions when your mum and dad are wrapped up in their own feelings or you think you might not get an honest answer – or the answer you would like to hear.

Some of these feelings can be very stressful and then it is difficult to imagine that you will feel differently one day. But children of divorce are not the only children who feel unhappy and miserable and lose confidence; the reasons may be different, but everyone, whether child or adult, goes through bad patches, and try to remember that things gets better.

You might give some thought to *happiness,* because it is easy to imagine everyone else is happy while you are miserable. Perhaps you think you don't deserve to be happy or it's no good trying because it won't last. Happiness doesn't have to be deserved or earned and you don't have to have a reason. You might think people will be sympathetic if you are miserable; some, maybe, but most would rather you were bright and interesting and interested in their lives.

To be happy is mostly an attitude to life, one you may have to pretend about before it becomes real. If you relax and smile and decide it's OK to be happy, it's OK to look forward, to make some goals, and, most important, to believe it's OK to feel good about yourself, then, in the end, you are more likely to be truly OK.

## Some Things You Might Have to Accept

The first can be hard; it is to accept that your parents are not likely to live together any more. To do so they would have to love each other again, which is not very likely after what has happened. They certainly would not want to carry on with the rows and difficulties which are not good for anyone. Some parents still care a lot for each other but know they simply can't live together happily.

Next, it is important to remember that it is never the children's fault when parents separate. They got together before children were involved, and when they separate it is about what they feel about each other. In other words, it is always about adult feelings.

Another thing to remember is that what happens is never all bad but you have to look for the good things and it is likely to be some time before things do improve. One good thing about parents living separately might be that they don't quarrel as much, and some children find that when parents live apart, they continue to be united over the children. You are really very lucky if, as sometimes happens, your parents become friendly with each other. Another is that despite the difficulties, such as not having so much money, they might be happier, and then you will be too. A cloud will have lifted from you and life will be good again.

## What You Might Do to Help Yourself

There are a lot of possible difficulties when parents separate, some of which are discussed below. They won't all apply to you, but it might be worth thinking about those which do.

You have to know when to pick the right time to ask questions. If you start to do this, you will find your confidence grows and you will be able to say what you would like to happen, without pleading or threatening, but clearly and honestly, showing that you have thought about the consequences of what you think. Of course you can't please everybody all the time and there are some important things adults have to decide, though they need to know what your feelings are about them.

You have to face inevitable losses – of stability, security, and perhaps trust in adults, as well as changes in your lifestyle – but you have to accept that there is nothing you or anyone else can do to change the past and you can only make changes in how you think and behave in the future. Nevertheless, if you can make some good changes then other people in your family might too.

If you are feeling awful, don't wait until things get even worse. Find an adult or someone you can trust who will listen to you and help you sort things out. You might talk to other children with separated parents who have some idea about how you are feeling. Another possibility is to see if there are groups for children (there aren't many around) or whether counselling for children is offered. This doesn't mean there is something wrong with you. A counsellor will listen and help you think aloud about what is in your mind. A doctor or the local Citizens' Advice Bureau should know what is available in your area for children. Another possibility, of course, is to ring ChildLine.

It is extra difficult if your parents continue arguing. If so, tell them firmly, without shouting or getting angry, that it upsets you, or walk away. You can play a positive part by separating yourself from the battles and refusing to take sides. It will probably take some courage but you might have to tell them, probably more than once, that you don't want to keep their secrets or be a messenger between them any more. You don't have to listen to nasty things they say about each other or repeat bad things you are told.

Most children worry about their parents. 'Will Dad manage on his own?'; 'Will he feed himself?'; 'Will Mum be lonely?'; 'How will she cope with doing the garden and mending things?' Remember, though, that adults are usually fairly tough and you can still be caring and supportive without taking responsibility on your own shoulders.

For a while, after the separation, parents are having to deal with their own painful feelings and may be not so concerned about their children as they were. Some appear to be angry about everything. This is temporary and will get better. Even if they don't love each other any more, this doesn't stop them loving you.

You are not a leaf in the wind being blown this way and that; you can make things happen and you can help make things better. It may well happen that because of what you've been through you will have more understanding of other people's feelings. This will be important if, for instance, a parent is unhappy; you can help by remembering that parents need some loving too and also by helping in small ways. For instance, you could make sure you return from contact visits on time and avoid making 'winding-up' remarks such as: 'Dad is going to buy me an expensive computer', or 'Mum lets me do it in her house.' You might take responsibility for doing your homework or perhaps in doing things about the house or making small changes, in order to reduce the little things which can cause trouble between parents and for which they blame each other.

It can be difficult visiting the parent you don't live with. Sometimes that parent thinks of you as you were when they separated and doesn't understand you are growing and changing. Some might think they have to spend lots of money on you, when really children just want to feel loved and special. Contact visits can be difficult – especially if you don't like fast food – and although it is nice to have treats, it doesn't have to be all the time. What you might really want is for Dad (or Mum) to treat you with respect (not do things you don't like, not criticize you or make put-down remarks, for instance), to be interested and caring, and sometimes if he has a new partner and she has her own children, to spend time with you on your own. You might have to explain to your parent what you really want in a loving way and as tactfully as you can without upsetting feelings, though this can be a very difficult thing to do.

Some children like a parent's new partner a lot, but others don't. You might feel you don't want another mum, for instance, or one who is trying to be your grown-up sister, but if Dad likes her maybe you could try to see her differently, not as the person who has stolen your dad. She hasn't, because the love he has for her is very different from the love he has for you, his child. It will take time to feel comfortable with each other and require a lot of understanding on both sides. You won't have the same feelings for her as those you have for your mum, but it will make life a lot easier for both of you if you can be friendly with each other, then perhaps you won't need to feel disloyal. But, like everything about divorce and separation, it's not easy.

Imagine Dad has a girlfriend called Jane whom you don't like so you are horrible to her. Maybe when Dad and Jane are together you feel left out and if she wasn't there you could have Dad to yourself, but perhaps you also think if you got to know her and like her, you would be being disloyal to Mum. If you could stop thinking like this then you might get to like her and she would get to like you. Wicked stepmothers belong to fairy stories. Sometimes it is difficult because if you are angry with Mum or Dad you feel they might stop loving you if they knew that, but sometimes if you keep the anger inside yourself you get pains and scary nightmares or don't want to do anything. The real reason might be that you are feeling *unloved*, and if this is so then it is better to ask for a hug than to hit someone.

It could be that Jane is all right but it is her children you can't deal with. If they are younger they get lots of attention from your dad or they may mess up your things and you feel when you are staying with them that you have no privacy. There might be a solution: it is better to think about what the solution might be and make a suggestion than to go around with a lot of resentment inside you.

Sometimes the problem is between Dad and Mum's new partner. Dad may worry that you will love Mum's new boyfriend or husband more than him, and he may make nasty remarks about the boyfriend. This can be very stressful, especially if this man is kind to you. You might need to tell your dad many times that he is your dad and special for you and it upsets you when he runs down other people. When you are with him, then only he matters to you and you want him to only think about you. Your dad might have forgotten that we all love people in many different ways.

**Things Get Better**

Finally, parents' divorce can be one of the worst things to happen to children, but the bad feelings don't last for ever. In time, most parents sort out their own problems and become more understanding of their children. These are some of the things that can happen:

- Children become more independent and learn to rely on themselves; and even if there is less money around, life usually becomes less stressful and some things are better. Children can play a part in achieving this.

- Parents see children as individuals and can get to know them in a new way. This can be appreciated by children once they begin to enjoy life again and see things more positively. They have to accept that being with Dad is different from being with Mum; there are different expectations, different rules and different things to enjoy.

- Divorce brings new changes and new challenges. Often, grown-ups do their best to help, but the children involved can help themselves, and, given time, feelings change. Children do have some power; they can make things happen. It takes courage, but things can and usually do improve.

There is a lot of living and learning and loving to be done. Start now!

# 15 Conclusion

The sheer number of children affected by the break-up of their parents' relationship is creating an enormous problem requiring imaginative solutions. These should not fail to take into consideration the two main themes of this book: that the views and opinions of children should be heard and respected and that there should be more appreciation of their feelings at this time. Numerous examples have demonstrated the importance of both points.

## What Can Be Done?

*Issues Relating Specifically to Children*
When decisions are being made about children's future, ways need to be found for their views and wishes to be heard directly, in a situation where they feel safe to voice such feelings; and they should be given information which they can understand and, if necessary, confidential help with their feelings at the time of the crisis. To involve children is a financially costly option requiring manpower, training and resources, but the likely long-term gains for their future mental health are immeasurable.

*Parenting After Separation*
At the time after separation, for the sake of the children it is important to end the hostility which properly belonged to the marriage. Because of the harm antagonism at the beginning and end of contact visits can do, it is in the children's interests that parental responsibility, which requires co-operation, is shared only when there is a measure of agreement between the parents. Where the hostility continues, decisions about parenting might be delayed until there is some civility between the parents, or be made for a limited period only, to see how the arrangements are working out and to ascertain the views of the children on this issue.

Once that matter is resolved, stability is needed. The requisite conditions have been well stated. According to one study: 'Our review convinced us that the most important factors in assuring the well-being of children after divorce are that the mother be an effective parent, providing love, nurturing, a predictable routine and consistent and moderate discipline and that the children not be exposed to continual conflict between the parents' (Furstenberg and Cherlin 1991, p. 118).

*What is Definitely Harmful*
Some situations which are generally accepted as being harmful to children with separated parents have been discussed throughout the book; among them are multiple changes in family composition, physical and sexual abuse and domestic violence, the absence of a parent, and social situations which stem largely from poverty and its effects. However, emotional abuse is largely ignored though it is more widespread, more insidious and often more difficult to detect; the methods for its discovery need to be refined. It is the antithesis of ensuring that a child's emotional needs are met.

*Parenting Methods*
Methods of parenting can have long-term consequences. One approach might be for the child to feel both loved and respected at all times and to know that parents see him as special; techniques would include benign limits consistently applied and the child being given appropriate choices, and receiving attention for non-naughty behaviour, followed by pleasure for acceptable approved acts.

Some ten-year-old children in one group maintained that their parents never made encouraging or approving remarks to or about them and they would be embarrassed if they did so. It is not surprising that they need the approval of their peers for what they possess or wear. How children are disciplined would be an important part of these changes. A regrettable example of what happens now was demonstrated by the announcement of a proposal that parents should no longer be permitted to beat their children, though they could continue to smack them (October 1998). Even small smacks have no place in this very different approach to helping a child accept limits and grow up happy and confident, whether with one parent or two.

More thought needs to be given to ensure that non-resident parents have the resources to make a long-term commitment and maintain contact, as this is usually in the best interests of the child. Some of them would probably welcome the opportunity to learn about successful parenting given the emotional and practical difficulties of being a lone parent. Fathers and mothers, whether resident or non-resident parent, might be glad of such support and encouragement.

If parenting is to be changed for the better it requires that the knowledge we now have be made more widely available. This would include information about children's development, their feelings and needs; the importance of the fathers' involvement with the children before and after separation; the harm certain actions can have on them and ways of disciplining which do not include physical pain. All these points are capable of contributing to a change in the way many children are seen and treated at present and are necessary if the idea of parental responsibilities rather than parental rights is to be more than a catchphrase.

The need for better parenting to improve children's lot is not limited to the divorce situation. One study using the National Children's Bureau cohort claimed: 'a substantial portion of what is usually considered the effect of divorce on children is visible before the parents separate', and, 'At least as much attention needs to be paid to the process that occurs in troubled intact families as to the trauma that children suffer after the parents separate' (Cherlin et al. 1991). The second quotation raises questions that are outside the scope of this book, but is relevant in showing that the distress of children in intact homes can also be considerable whether parents separate later, or not.

*Wider issues*
At the moment there is a division between those married with children, on the one hand, and partners with children, on the other, the second group being largely ignored. A more logical division would be between couples with children and those without, especially concerning divorce proceedings.

As far as children are concerned the government would need to rethink priorities and address the low standard of resources for children. The provision of good experiences for young children; for example, by encouraging and providing resources for the expansion of schemes such as Newpin and Homestart, High Scope nurseries (O'Flaherty 1995) and nurture groups in schools (Bennathan and Boxall 1996) would be a good contribution to improving the situation. Older children could be taught about strategies to deal with conflict, and what is necessary to maintain close relationships and to prevent their break-up, involving both boys and girls. But parenting skills and the importance of children's needs should not be ignored.

The government is introducing schemes to provide the resources for training, afterschool provision and work for lone parents, but more consideration should be given to improving the financial situation for them so that families with children are not brought up in substandard surroundings without the basic necessities. Encouragement to employers to play a larger part by providing flexible working hours and childcare provision could be part of the solution.

Another important aspect of social change, one that affects children greatly, concerns the role of men. 'Macho man' has lost or is losing his place, but while he has taken on domestic tasks, he has not so far been too happy with sharing some of the emotional tasks of the family. The number of those able to do this and to be involved with the upbringing of their children from the start is increasing, greatly to the benefit of their children. The problem now is to address the reluctance of many men who are uncomfortable with showing warm feelings verbally as well as physically, and who therefore tend to opt out of situations where children need a demonstration of adults' care and concern.

To achieve such a fundamental change is an enormous task, and one that can only be done very gradually. It entails giving men the confidence to learn about children's needs and so be supportive parents for their children. Fathers who are concerned about their self-esteem will enrich their own and their children's life and actually enjoy them. They also have to learn how to provide benign limits. As a spin-off they would make a considerable contribution to keeping their youngsters out of trouble. Lone fathers, as well as those living with their families, have an important challenge to meet which involves their being both strong and sensitive.

An even broader social change would be for children to be accepted and enjoyed as they are in some other countries. Anyone who has observed how small children are welcomed in, say, French or Italian restaurants and has contrasted it with their reception in many British establishments, will understand what is meant by this. Children have to be appreciated for themselves far more than at present. This may be the underlying reason why in so many of the European league tables which involve children, Britain is so often near the bottom.

## A Good Divorce for Children

Despite the trauma and stress experienced by most children whose parents divorce or separate, my hope is that the message conveyed by this book is that if children know they are valued by both parents, if their feelings are not forgotten and good parenting continues despite the trauma which affects everyone in the family, then the break-up does not have to be a disastrous experience for them. There *is* such a thing as 'a good divorce' for children.

# Bibliography

Place of publication is London unless otherwise stated.

Amato, P.R. and Keith, B. (1991) 'Parental divorce and the well-being of children: a meta-analysis', *Psychological Bulletin* 110(1), 26–46.

Ayalon, O. and Flasher, A. (1993) *Chain Reaction: Children and Divorce*. Kingsley.

Bannister, A. (1997) *The Healing Drama*. Free Association Books.

Beal, E.W. and Hochman, G. (1991) *Adult Children of Divorce; How to Achieve Happier Relationships*. Piatkus.

Bennathan, M. and Boxall, M. (1996) *Effective Intervention in Primary Schools: Nurture Groups*. David Fulton.

Bertoia, C.E. and Drakich, J. (1995) 'The Fathers' Rights movement; contradictions in rhetoric and practice', in W. Marsiglio (ed.), *Fatherhood: Contemporary Theory, Research and Society Policy*. Newbury Park, CA: Sage, pp. 230–54.

Burghes, L. (1994) *Lone Parenthood and Family Disruption*. Family Policy Studies Occasional Papers 18. Family Policy Studies Centre.

Cherlin, A.J., Furstenberg, F.F., Chase-Lansdale, P.L., Kiernan, K., Robins, P.K., Morrison, D.R. and Teitler, J.O. (1991) 'Longitudinal studies of the effects of divorce on children in Great Britain and the United States', *Science* 252, 1386–9.

ChildLine (1998) *Unhappy Families, Unhappy Children*, ChildLine.

Child Poverty Action Group (1998) *Real Choices for Lone Parents and their Children*. CPAG.

Clark, D. (1989) *Representing Children*. Kent and Sussex Independent Counselling Agency.

Clulow, C. and Vincent, C. (1987) *In the Child's Best Interests*. Tavistock.

Cockett, M. and Tripp, J. (1994) *The Exeter Family Study: Family Breakdown and its Impact on Children*. Exeter: University of Exeter Press.

Dominian J., Mansfield, P., Dormor, D. and McAllister, F. (1991) *Marital Breakdown and the Health of the Nation*. One plus One – Marriage and Partnership Research.

Elliott, B. J. and Richards, M.P.M. (1991), 'Effects of parental divorce on children', *Archives of Disease in Childhood* 66, 915–16.

Furstenberg, F. and Cherlin, A. (1991) *Divided Families: What Happens to Children When Parents Part*. Cambridge MA: Harvard University Press.

Gorill Barnes, G., Thompson, P. and Burchardt, N. (eds) (1998) *Growing Up in Stepfamilies*. Oxford: Oxford University Press.

Gottman, J. (1991) *The Heart of Parenting*. Bloomsbury.

Gray, B. (1998) 'Intake and criminal record checks', *Family Mediation*, 8(2), 5.

Herefordshire Family Mediation (1996) 'Children and mediation', *Family Mediation*, 6(3), 14–15.

Hester, M. and Pearson, C. (1993) 'Domestic violence, mediation and child contract arrangements: issues from current research', *Family Mediation* 3(2), 3–6.

Hetherington, E.M. (1989) 'Coping with family transitions: winners, losers and survivors', *Child Development*, 60, 1–14.

Hooper, C.A. (1994) 'Do families need fathers? The impact of divorce on children' in A. Mullender and R. Morley (eds), *Children Living With Domestic Violence*. Whiting and Birch, pp. 86–101.

Ironside, V. (1996) *The Huge Bag of Worries*. MacDonald.

Jaffe, P. et al. (1990) *Children of Battered Women*. Newbury Park, CA; London: Sage.

James, G. (1994) *Discussion Report for the Area Child Protection Committee Conference: Study of Working Together 'Part 8' Reports*. Department of Health ACPO Series, Report No. 1.

Jewett, C. (1997) *Helping Children with Separation and Loss*, 2nd edn. Free Association Books.

Kaufman J. and Zigler, E. (1987) 'Do abused children become abusive parents?', *American Journal of Orthopsychiatry*, 57 (2), 186–92.

Kaye, M. (1996) 'Domestic violence, residence and contact', *Child and Family Law Quarterly*, 8, 285–96.

Kelly, J. (1993) 'Current research on children's post-divorce adjustment: no simple answers', *Family and Conciliation Courts Review*, 31, 29–49.

Kelly, L. (1994) 'The interconnectedness of domestic violence and child abuse: challenges for research, policy and practice', in A. Mullender and R. Morley (eds), *Children Living With Domestic Violence*. Whiting and Birch, pp. 43–56.

Kiernan, K. (1991) What about the children? *Family Policy Studies Bulletin*, December.

MacDermott, T. et al. (1998) *Real Choices for Lone Parents and Their Children*. Child Poverty Action Group.

MacLeod, M. (1996) *Talking With Children About Child Abuse*. ChildLine.

McCarthy, P. and Walker, J. (1996) 'The long-term impact and family mediation', *Childright* 131, 13–16.

Mitchell, A.K. (1985) *Children in the Middle: Living Through Divorce.* Tavistock.

Morley, R. and Mullender, A. (1994) 'Domestic violence and children: what do we know from research?' in A. Mullender and R. Morley (eds), *Children Living With Domestic Violence.* Whiting and Birch, pp. 24–42.

O'Flaherty, J. (1995) *Intervention in the Early Years: An Evaluation of the High/Scope Curriculum.* National Children's Bureau/Barnardo.

Pincus, L. and Dare, C. (1978) *Secrets in the Family.* New York: Pantheon.

Rodgers, B. and Pryor, J. (1998) *Divorce and Separation: the Outcomes for Children.* York: Joseph Rowntree Foundation.

Rowlands, P. (1980) *Saturday Parent.* Allen and Unwin.

Rutter, M. and Madge, N. (1976) *Cycles of Disadvantage.* Heinemann.

Rutter, M. and Rutter M. (1972) *Developing Minds.* Harmondsworth: Penguin.

Saunders, A. (1995) *'It Hurts Me Too': Children's Experience of Domestic Violence and Refuge Life.* Women's Aid Federation England, National Institute for Social Work, ChildLine.

Smart, C. and Neale, B. (1998) *Family Fragments.* Oxford: Polity Press.

Smith, H. (1995) *Unhappy Children: Reasons and Remedies.* Free Association Books.

Stark, E. and Flitcraft, A. (1985) 'Woman-battering, child abuse and social heredity: what is the relationship?', in N. Johnson, *Marital Violence.* Routledge and Kegan Paul.

*UN Human Development Report 1998,* abstract in *Poverty: Journal of the Child Poverty Action Group* 101, 17–18.

Walker, J. (1993) 'Parenting after separation'. Unpublished paper presented at the Joseph Rowntree Foundation seminar, London, November.

Wallerstein, J. (1988) 'Children of divorce: the dilemma of a decade' in E.W. Nunnelly, C.S. Chilman and F.M. Cox (eds), *Troubled Relationships.* Newbury Park, CA; London: Sage, pp. 55–73.

Wells, R. (1993) *Helping Children Cope with Divorce* (rev. edn). Sheldon.

Winnicott, C. (1968) 'Communicating with children' in R.J.N. Tod (ed.), *Disturbed Children.* Longman.

Winnicott, D.W. (1971) *Playing and Reality.* Tavistock.

Wolfe, D.A. et al. (1985) 'Children of battered women; the relation of child behaviour to family violence and maternal stress', *Journal of Consulting and Clinical Psychology* 53, 657–65.

# Index